Blooming Happya®

Grow, Flourish and Thrive

Beyond Survival

Clare Deacon

AND CO.

Disclaimer

This book is not intended to be an alternative to seeking mental health support. If you or someone you know is struggling, please seek appropriate support from your GP. Listed in the back of this book are some other resources that can help you and are there to listen in confidence.

———

CONTENTS

H A P P Y A®

HAP-PEE-UH

Your unique recipe of happiness and contentment for living in alignment with your true self. Achieving a sense of inner contentment, where clarity, purpose, fulfilment, and joy intertwine to create a lasting and enriched sense of well-being. It's a state far beyond survival.

GROW

Expanding your knowledge and honing your skills. Nurturing the seeds of your true self. Being intentional about the continuous development of your authentic self.

Flourish

Beyond growth, a vibrant blossoming of your being in a way that brings about a deep sense of fulfilment and prosperity. Not only aligning with your true self but experiencing the abundance of a happya life.

Thrive

Where you not only experience growth and flourishing but also excel in the different areas of your life, embracing challenges, and reaching high levels of success.

DEDICATION

This book is dedicated to the fearless warriors who've embarked on a journey where survival alone isn't enough; to those who we've lost along the way, for whom holding on became a battle they could no longer fight; to those who've boldly faced challenges and battled their inner critics; and to all those who have been a part of my own journey and who always believed in me.

Thank you. Thank you for being the driving force in my search for happya, for inspiring me to seek more and for proving that "more" was within reach.

In loving memory of Dave, my Superman, my eternal superhero, forever in my heart and always by my side. To Jerry, a beacon of light when the world seemed so very dark and Wendy, who never failed to raise my spirits with a cuppa and a chat. The world is a darker place without you.

To my amazing children, you are an endless source of inspiration, overflowing with kindness, love, and talent. I am profoundly proud and fortunate to have the honour of being your mum.

Thank you to everyone who has been a part of my happya journey, past and present, and to all those who I am yet to meet as I continue my happya journey.

With love and gratitude

Clare xx

Clare Deacon

Author Blooming Happya: Grow, Flourish, Thrive – Beyond Survival

Founder of Happya Ltd.

PREFACE

Welcome to a journey unlike any other – a journey that navigates the unique blend of all that is you, beyond your past and the shadows of survival, out of the darkness and into the radiant light of your happya. Happya is your unique recipe of happiness and contentment, for living in alignment with your true self. Finding your happya enables you to achieve a sense of inner contentment, where clarity, purpose, fulfilment and joy intertwine to create a lasting and enriched sense of wellbeing. It's a state far beyond that of survival. This book provides a pathway for anyone who's spent a lifetime holding on, but who knows that, for them, survival isn't enough.

In these pages, you will embark on a transformational journey, founded in the science of positive psychology, providing an alternative to the illness ideology of the mental health system that can leave you stuck in the shadow of trauma.

Life often places us in circumstances where survival seemingly becomes our only option. It keeps us safe when we need it the most.

The trials we face, the wounds we carry, and the adversities we overcome can shape the fabric of our existence. But your story extends far beyond survival. You have the power within you to write the next chapter of your life; trauma and survival are not the end of your story. Within you lies the potential to live your happya life.

This book is an invitation to rediscover yourself at the root of who you really are. An invitation to go beyond the limitations of survival and achieve transformative growth towards happya. The opening chapters prepare you for the happya journey ahead by equipping you with an understanding of where you are and the journey you have travelled to date. It continues along a pathway illuminated by the six guiding lights: Harmonise Your Authenticity, Acknowledge Your Emotions, Preserve Your space, Process and Release, Yes to Your Dreams, and Activate Your Life. Each of these lights represents a fundamental step in your journey of self-discovery, growth and healing.

As you delve into the pages ahead, you will find an approach that has been constructed from science, wisdom, experience, and the profound insights of those who have walked the path before you. This is not just a book; it is a toolkit, a roadmap, and a companion to accompany you through the challenges and triumphs that lie ahead.

Your journey begins now. Together, let's journey to the root of you so you can be blooming happya, beyond survival where you can grow, flourish, and thrive.

"On the other side of a storm is the strength that comes from having navigated through it. Raise your sail and begin."

— GREGORY S. WILLIAM

Introduction
Embarking on Your Journey to Happya

Ever felt like you don't belong? Ever felt like you should be more, you should be better, you should be "practically perfect in every way"? Do you spend time daydreaming about a life that seems to have passed you by? Perhaps you feel as though you have woken up and are living someone else's life, uncertain how you got here or indeed, where you left the person you used to be. Whatever happened to that dream you had?

If you find yourself wanting to stop the roller coaster of life and pause for just a second so you can gain your bearings, this book is for you. It's for you if you struggle to uphold your boundaries, if you find yourself constantly people-pleasing, or are frustrated with your life but just don't seem able to make that change. It's for you if you don't feel worthy to ask for what you want or need. Perhaps you're not even sure what you would ask for. If you feel you are the root of the problem, if you feel guilt and shame for wanting more, for wanting something different, this book is here for you. It's a place where you can feel heard and know you are not alone.

Perhaps you are already living a dream life. Nevertheless, your presence is welcome wholeheartedly, for at your core, regardless of your journey, there inevitably remains the allure of pursuing the next aspiration or conquering a fresh challenge. Your insatiable desires are inherent, continually propelling you forward.

Ultimately, if you've been yearning to feel heard and to be seen for who you really are, if you need help in finding that version of yourself, I am here for you. And here is the secret that only those who complete the journey really get to understand... *you* are not broken. For all you are and all you are not, you are a beautiful and fabulous human with so much to offer.

You are beautiful for being the complex version of yourself, your whole self. You are completely normal whilst, at the same time, you are entirely unique, just like everyone else. Normal, according to the Cambridge Dictionary means ordinary or usual. Your feelings, your emotions, your behaviours, and your actions are all normal - normal for the set of beliefs you hold. Normal for your personality. Normal for the situation and circumstances you are in and normal for chapters of your story and the path you have walked. But if you are looking for your normal to look and feel different to what it does right now, then that is something we can achieve together.

You may need to hold onto the faith that you are not broken, there is hope and with the right mindset, tools and approaches you can achieve anything you want, but you are going to have to be honest with yourself and with the universe, learn to ask for what you want, recognise your needs in achieving all of this and to give your commitment to the work that's needed.

Are you ready to do that?

You do not have to do this alone. It doesn't matter how far you have or haven't come. It's about who you are in the here and now, helping you make the decision that survival isn't enough and embarking on a journey to find your happya. It's about addressing those feelings of discomfort and releasing trauma, fulfilling that desire for something more. It's about managing the fear of failure so that one day, you will wake up without the "could have", "should have" spiral of shame.

If you're not quite sure you can, here's the thing: I believe in you, and I believe in the reality of achieving your vision even if you have no idea what that looks like right now. I know some of you are going to be sceptical and I get that (I was too when I first started my recovery and transformation journey) but there is a version of you that needs to do this; the version of you that wants more, who deserves to be happy, to feel confident and loved. Allow them to be heard, allow that version of you to take the lead.

Some of you will feel that perhaps you are just not deserving enough, which I'm afraid I'm going to call BS on. That stuff, those thoughts, that narrative needs to be released. If you decide to follow this journey, you are going to be able to banish them to the chapters of the past. In the meantime, when you don't feel enough when you don't have the capacity to do it, I am here for you, to guide you and to hold space for you.

To be seen and to be heard, there is going to be a requirement for you to be honest and open with who you are and that might just be too much of a vulnerable place for you to start. If that's the case, then what I ask of you right now is simply to sit tight and listen, allow the words on the page to float around your brain and see where you land. Alternatively, seek the professional support you need.

Now, this book is very much not about me, but I get it; before you can really open up on this journey, you first need to put your trust in me. You have already shown me some faith in getting this far and for that, I am grateful. You see, not only are you taking a step towards finding your own happya, but you are also part of a story where a six-year-old girl was once told she wasn't any good at story writing and could never dream of being an author. The same person who faced adversity and trauma made the decision to embark on a transformative journey and found her passion in using all she had experienced to help others and invested in equipping herself with the skills and expertise so that she could be assured of her own transformation. You are all a part of my journey to finding my happya, and I am very honoured to have you here.

I spent a lifetime living in a world where I didn't feel I belonged. I certainly didn't feel I fit in. I had a constant feeling I was in the wrong room, a feeling that I was attending a party I hadn't been invited to. I developed a long list of all the ways in which I was too much, further compounded by the backup list of all the ways in which I was also not enough. I allowed very few people to see the real me (I can count them on one hand with fingers to spare). I was a closed book. I'm sure many of you can resonate with those feelings of being lost, of not belonging, of being judged and feeling you had to protect yourself by hiding.

I grew up in a household of domestic violence and abuse; my family was dysfunctional, a fact I had to hide from the outside world, including my friends because I was supposedly part of a world where "things like that" don't happen. Friends never caught on that I was always up for a sleepover because I couldn't face going home, especially once my siblings jumped ship. By the age of fifteen, I was effectively sofa surfing. I had a part-time job which enabled me to have a good social life and somehow, I managed to negotiate school, work and socialising, to survive and avoid my "home" life. By the time I was at college, it was all taking its toll, but I had one person who saw my pain, who never asked questions of me but gave me space to be heard when I needed it. He was the first person who showed faith in me, who saw me for who I really was and recognised my potential. It was only later in life I understood the reason he was able to identify my inner turmoil was because of his own.

By the time I was seventeen, my family had imploded. Our home was repossessed, my dad was sectioned, and my world was in disarray. I survived that dysfunction and made my escape to university where I was able to just be me, but I was unknowingly stuck in a survival mode with all I had experienced. My walls were built thick and strong to hide the dysfunction and I created a new life.

University allowed me to take some control of my life and it is where I met my future husband. Life continued to throw some curveballs, but I managed to survive by hiding my emotions. As a child, I'd learned conforming was important to survive. I built a successful career, married my handsome husband, and had three beautiful children and a nice home.

Whilst I believed I was conforming, the people from those past chapters often saw me as quite the opposite. Let me explain. Whilst I ticked the boxes of what I felt I "should" do, I often did them in a slightly different way or could be seen to antagonise along the way. I'm quite sure my headmaster and a few of my work colleagues would attest to that!

You see, given my experiences growing up, I was a rebel against the patriarchy but at the same time, I felt standing up for myself wasn't safe. I'd learned if you spoke out of line, there were consequences. I was caught somewhere between wanting to change the world and just wanting to hide, and in many ways, I was successful in doing both, which is what probably led me to wonder whether I was bipolar. I thought there was something wrong with me for not feeling fulfilled. I put up with how my world had been pieced together and whilst there was a lot to be grateful for, there were also things I accepted because of my low self-worth, lack of self-love, and the fact I was unknowingly stuck in survival mode.

We lived a comfortable life. We had our dramas, as all couples do, and life sent us some curveballs, but nothing prepared me for what was to come. One day, without warning, my husband unexpectedly had a cardiac arrest and died, at home, whilst our children slept upstairs. In the space of an hour, my world had changed from sitting on the sofa, ready to watch the latest episode of *Cold Feet*, to a room of friends and family, grieving and in shock, with blue lights lighting up the street. He was gone. My world was shattered. the one person I had been able to rely on, who was safe, was no longer there. The most devastating part is I couldn't protect my babies from the heartbreak. There is no greater feeling of failure than having to be a parent who drains the magic out of your children's faces by telling them the hardest truth of them all – their world isn't safe.

I had worked so hard to do things right and yet still the universe had decided it wasn't enough; that I wasn't enough to warrant the world we had created.

The following weeks were mind-numbingly painful; I was in emotional turmoil and yet the world seemed to be demanding even more from me. I had no idea how I was supposed to behave. I was trying to do my very best to honour my husband's memory, to support my children, to answer friends and family and to do it all without falling apart. The journey of being widowed is one I will save for a different time but to give context, here are some of the key moments so you can understand how I started my journey of recovery and beyond and how that enables me to help you with yours.

The first of those moments was the promise I made to my husband after he passed. Sat with him in the back of the ambulance outside our home, I promised that whilst I didn't know how, I was going to do my best to keep our dreams for our children alive, that his legacy wouldn't be a broken family.

The next was in the weeks after the funeral when the children were all back at school and everyone else had seemingly gone back to their own lives. I found myself falling into a state of real darkness and one day, that got too dark. I knew I was slipping too far, and I had to sound the alarm for help. I was lucky enough that someone came running. It was then I made the choice that if I was going to keep my promise to my husband, if I was going to do this, then it was going to be for so much more than survival. I had wasted so much time being stuck in survival mode. I hadn't fought all my life to lose the war now. And in any case, what could the universe really throw at me now? It had already destroyed everything. I made a commitment that I was going to try anything and everything I could to find happiness for myself and my children.

As the weeks and months passed, I found myself at work, the children at school and whilst a dark cloud overshadowed our house, a routine was forming; a routine I realised I didn't want and hadn't wanted for a long time. I sat in what felt like the same meeting, played over and over again, having the same debates and being treated the same way only now I was considered broken because my husband had died. I knew I wanted out but what else was I going to do? I made the decision to quit my job. I walked out on almost twenty years of corporate life, against the judgement of everyone around me, with absolutely no clue what I was going to do but simply knowing that it wasn't what I wanted and there had to be more. If I was going to live my life, it had to be for more. No longer was I hiding, no longer was I going to accept a life of survival.

I immersed myself in family life. We spent a year having fun, visiting friends and going on adventures. I feel extremely privileged that I was able to have that time. We also did the hard work; we went to counselling, tried different therapies and embraced life. However, I couldn't do that forever. I needed to find a future, but it had to fill me with joy. I needed to find my passion.

I had no idea where to start so I focused on what did light me up and I returned to university to study psychology to understand the science behind the transformation that was taking place for me and my family. As I sat in a lecture on trauma and was introduced to the concept of post-traumatic growth, I almost leapt out of my chair – that was it! That is what I was experiencing! I couldn't believe my ears! It tied together my therapy and recovery to explain my transformation and made me realise "I am normal!" My behaviour, actions and beliefs were not because I was dysfunctional; it was because I was holding onto trauma. I wasn't broken. I didn't need fixing. I needed some compassion and to heal from the decades of trauma. I felt supercharged. I had the answer. I needed to equip myself with the skills and experience so I could show others the way. And right there, in that lecture room, is where the first concept of happya was born.

I specialised in positive psychology, and focused on post-traumatic growth gained my master's degree. I trained as a counsellor and qualified in therapeutic skills including hypnotherapy and emotional freedom technique. If you want the whole list of qualifications, you can check out my website, www.happya-coach.com.

My own transformation set the foundations of my business and the values I uphold. You see, the thing is there were so many points in my journey where I could have become lost, and I am grateful I had the resources and opportunities I did. It was a difficult journey and still is, some days. It's an ongoing exploration as I continue my personal growth journey.

A journey of transformation is not easy and there are several potential pitfalls, but I am here to help you navigate through them. The key to success for me was finding ethical, trained professionals to support me because there are a lot of so-called professionals operating without any, or very few, qualifications. Were you aware that anyone in the UK can call themselves a psychologist, therapist, counsellor or coach? None of these terms are protected. Do you really want to be working with an individual who has no formal training, who does not adhere to an ethical code of practice and who is unlikely to hold insurance?

What is the difference between a counsellor and a coach?

Well, a counsellor, despite common perceptions, is not someone focused solely on the past (although this is the case for most clients). Counselling focuses on an individual's psychological well-being and interpersonal relationships. It addresses psychological distress.

A coach is developmental in nature and looks at change and taking action. They support you in the achievement of your goals. A coach is there to guide; they don't offer solutions but facilitate the process. If you are looking for someone to give you answers, then you are probably looking for a mentor and should find an expert in the specific topic you are interested in.

There are pros and cons to each and, depending on where you currently find yourself, what you intend to achieve can greatly influence which of these is right for you. I decided to take a different approach in my training after my own therapist told me she was unable to support me with building my future life and I'd need to find myself a life coach. It brought back feelings of abandonment. I didn't want to start over again. I had come so far on the journey that I wanted to keep going and the thought of having to go through my story with someone else was just too overwhelming. Clients often come to me uncertain of what they really need because if it was that simple, they would have done it already. To ensure I get the best results and don't leave my clients stuck or feeling abandoned, I use a combined approach and adapt according to their personal needs.

I take the positive psychology approach because fundamentally, our mental health system is founded on an outdated illness ideology which reinforces distress and dysfunction, resulting in people often finding themselves stuck in a swamp of trauma recall. I hear endless cases of people giving up on therapy and counselling because it isn't working for them. I see the damage that is caused by coaches who are not qualified to deal with trauma and are not trained in counselling or therapy. Unlike traditional approaches, positive psychology offers a unique perspective on healing. It seeks to enhance well-being and help you thrive, even in the face of adversity. In healing from trauma, it focuses on leveraging your strengths, cultivating positive emotions, promoting resilience, and fostering personal growth. Through this approach, trauma survivors can not only recover but also thrive and find a renewed sense of purpose and well-being.

Given these insights, are you ready to make the decision that survival is no longer enough? Are you ready to let go of all that shame and guilt, and to say goodbye to the overwhelm and people-pleasing? Are you ready to say goodbye to your lack of self-belief and confidence, to come out of hiding and start showing up as who you really are? Are you ready to fulfil your destiny and live the life you deserve?

In the coming pages, you will embark on a transformative journey as I guide you to living a happya life. It is a journey of transformation towards a life of authenticity, self-care, and purpose - a life filled with joy and fulfilment. Together, we'll explore the depths of your true self by unlocking your story, passions and values. By nurturing a belief in your abilities to find your happya life you will lay the foundations of self-discovery, self-acceptance and empowerment.

Let's elevate your self-awareness, fortify your self-worth and nurture your confidence as we delve into the realm of self-care. Through these practices, you will cultivate a focused, more serene mind and attain the clarity you seek as to what joy and happiness look like for you.

As we navigate the process of releasing trauma and unlocking your limiting beliefs, we will, together, embrace emotional healing and bid farewell to the thoughts that are no longer serving you.

Your sense of safety and survival is found in your environment and being part of a community. But what if that community is not holding you up but, in fact, holding you back? It's time to build a circle of supporters, a network of cheerleaders who will uplift and inspire. However, your community can only do this when you uphold healthy boundaries which are communicated with love and kindness.

Having laid the foundations, it's time to dream and envision your future. Through conscious choices and intentional steps, you can take charge of your narrative and propel yourself forward with unwavering determination.

It will challenge you. You will need to face your fears, and you are going to need to have faith in me, the science, and yourself. It's going to require you to be brave and honest. If you want to make a difference in your life, you need to start showing up for the things you want and let go of what is no longer serving you.

Take a moment to visualise how it would feel to be living your happya life. Take a deep breath and consider how you want to think, feel, and behave. What difference would it make to you and the people you love? What would it be worth for you to have that feeling every day? What would you give to wake up knowing who you are, believing you are worthy, loving yourself and showing yourself some compassion? Because you are worth it. I know because you are a beautiful person, and you deserve to blossom and grow and live the life that you want to. Take a few moments to allow those thoughts and feelings to sink into your body.

Are you ready to reclaim your life and step into your full potential? Or are you going to continue being last on your to-do list, prioritising everyone else's needs over your own? Unless you treat yourself with love and compassion, others won't either and if you have children, they will be watching and learning from you. There's a reason on an aeroplane you're told to put your oxygen mask on first. If you've passed out, you aren't going to help anyone.

Delve into, Blooming Happya: Grow, Flourish, Thrive. Beyond Survival, as we unravel the real you, the version that has been hidden for so long. It's your time to transcend from mere survival to unlock the life you deserve, a life of purpose, joy and empowerment. Let's find your happya, your own unique recipe to happiness and contentment for living in alignment with your true self.

"I can and I will. Watch me."

— CARRIE GREEN

CHAPTER 1

STEPPING INTO CHANGE

Welcome! It's great to have you onboard. This journey will, at times, make you feel uncomfortable, but it is from discomfort that growth comes and that is what you are looking for. Ready? Let's do this.

In the first part of this book, it's time for you to find acceptance of who you are and begin to uncover the power there is within you, enabling the process of embracing your authentic self. The version of you that has been buried beneath others' needs and wants, underneath their expectations of who you should be. Ultimately, it's time to embrace your emotions, thoughts, and dreams as you explore feelings of self-worth and self-love and establish an authentic connection with the world around you. In this chapter, you will begin to get a sense of your current situation and an appreciation of why you have found yourself stuck. It is only when you acknowledge the status quo with an open mind and make a commitment to do something differently that change can happen.

Firstly, if, or should I say when, this raises feelings of discomfort, recognise it as a good sign; it's an indication of change and remember, that's the reason you invested in this book. You are looking for change, something different or perhaps you are aiming to step up your life to the next level. Either way, change is good. It's about becoming comfortable with it. If you are having some jelly wobbles (discomfort) then that's okay because you've got this and when you need a little more support, this book is here as your guide.

Let's explore for a moment the concept of discomfort and the acknowledgement of change. For some, feelings of change bring about excitement whilst for others it brings up fear. The truth about fear and excitement is that they feel very similar - it's our interpretation of those feelings as to whether they get labelled good or bad.

Think about a roller coaster ride. Some people will feel exhilaration; the thought of the sharp turns and stomach-flipping dips will be something to enjoy. For others, the experience sparks fear and is associated with a lack of control and danger. What's the difference between the two? The roller coaster is the same, the day is the same and the ride is going to be the same, so what's different? The difference is your interpretation of risk - how you rate the danger, or how safe you feel. It's about how the story is playing out in your mind, the consequences, and the potential outcome. For those who enjoy the roller coaster, their belief is that fundamentally, they are safe. It's a moment in time. It's not going to cause any negative consequences so they can enjoy the myriad of sensations that come their way and they interpret the stomach flip as excitement.

For others, that roller coaster represents danger, and a lack of control and is proceeded by a series of "what ifs". What if it breaks down? What if the bolts give way? What if my harness isn't secure? What if I'm sick? What if it hurts? What if I can't cope and want to get off? This spiral of negative thinking fills you with those same sensations but this time they are interpreted as being bad and it's time to run and get yourself to safety. It's worth highlighting that this narrative may be restricted to your subconscious, your body responds to all the negative messages even though your rational brain is saying that all is safe and well. This causes a conflict between how you are feeling and what you want, resulting in confusion and frustration.

Our thoughts and our inner narrative have a significant impact on our well-being and our success in life. As the quote from Henry Ford highlights "Whether you think you can, or you think you can't – you're right," which is supported through scientific research.

When studying for my master's I was determined to uncover how some people experience what is termed post-traumatic growth whilst others find themselves stuck and lost unable to move forward, termed *learned helplessness*. For those who experience post-traumatic growth, recovery from trauma is transformational and results in a positive impact on their overall well-being, whilst others, who are unable to recover may continue to see a decline in their well-being. Understanding the catalyst between the different outcomes enables us to understand the actions needed to enable recovery from trauma to take place and to find your happya, a concept we will dive into in the next chapter.

By exploring the psychology archives and conducting my own scientific research with survivors of trauma, I have been able to uncover a truth. Science has shown that those who believe they are a mere subject to the consequences of life, unable to influence outcomes, are more likely to experience feelings of helplessness and have lower satisfaction in life and well-being. Those who believe in their ability to influence outcomes experience a positive psychological transformation and gain an increased level of well-being and overall satisfaction with life. Whilst other factors may influence the speed of recovery, the fundamental difference, irrelevant to other factors, is whether a person believes they can determine their fate. There is a direct correlation between the belief you hold in yourself and your recovery.

Ultimately, the outcome, whether an individual achieves positive transformation or falls into a state of learned helplessness, is dependent on where you believe the power for change lies. If you leave it up to fate, the universe or someone else, it is unlikely you will experience positive emotions and attachment to the life you are currently living leaving you stuck. Whereas if *you* take control and harness your inner strength, believing that you can make a difference, the result is a happya you, a greater sense of satisfaction with life and inevitably, greater success. It doesn't mean you get to avoid trauma – unfortunately, nobody manages to escape that one -= but it does mean that it is less likely to prohibit you from ever living a happya life. The happya approach has been developed based on scientific evidence to support you to go beyond survival.

Why is this the case? Why does it make a difference what you believe? Fundamentally, if you believe you can't do something, you won't. You won't put in the effort, you won't take the necessary actions, you will inadvertently sabotage yourself and will be blind to opportunities to make change. It is equivalent to believing you have a predetermined destiny - like a pebble in the ocean, you must roll with the tides. However, if you make the decision to do something different, to believe in your own power for change, that you can make something happen, then inevitably, you will take the action you need and you will be open to opportunities that come your way.

Inevitably, there will be times in your life when you have taken decisive action, times when you have wanted something so badly that you have taken bold and decisive action and you have made it happen for yourself. Take a moment now to think about when you have made the decision to make something happen - it doesn't have to be newsworthy, but it must be something that you truly felt you wanted enough that it made you go all the way to achieving it. I doubt you started out thinking you were not able to achieve it, even though you knew there was a possibility you may not achieve it. It is harnessing that hope, the possibility of something different, that takes you to the next level.

Perhaps some of you have been working towards something and you never seem to quite manage it, perhaps you consider yourself to be a failure, but here's the thing, you only get to fail when you give up. In the meantime, you are learning how not to do it and if you harness that learning, you find growth and that is where the answer lies, if you keep working at it, you will achieve success. Let's start to reframe all those negative statements of *"I can't..."*, and *"I haven't"*, by ending them with *yet*. *"I can't... yet"*, *"I haven't found my happya yet."* These are all things you will be exploring throughout the pages of this book.

Your tendency to believe you can or believe you can't will be determined by your identity. Your identity refers to the characteristics, beliefs, values, roles, and affiliations that provide you with your sense of self. Your identity is also shaped through personal experiences - the stories you were told, and the expectations placed upon you by your community of advisors, invited or not. From conception, you are subject to different experiences, both positive and negative. There will be a set of expectations both knowingly and unknowingly placed upon you, a sense of right and wrong, that whole list of things you should do... And those you shouldn't. Quite often, you aren't even aware that you have taken on board these beliefs and have never actually stopped to consider whether they are what you want.

How many habits, rituals and ways of living your life did you proactively decide upon and how many of them have you inherited and accepted as yours because that's just how it's meant to be? Throughout this process, it's important to challenge yourself to dig deep and question whether the expectations, dreams and desires are founded on what you really want or whether it comes from an unconscious belief. When you find yourself saying I can't do that/have that/achieve that, challenge yourself to ask why not? When you find yourself saying you must do something/have something, ask yourself why and if you can't answer the why, perhaps it's not really what you want. Consider the difference it will make to your overall sense of satisfaction in life - by achieving a particular desire, what will be the outcome? Sometimes we want things, but we never take the time to really explore why or what need they are servicing.

As you begin to challenge some of the things in your life, you will inevitably encounter some resistance - after all, part of the brain's purpose is to ensure your survival and its belief is that if you survived last week doing what you did, then that is the safest course of action this week. Often, this results in the inner critic raising their voice and challenging why you are doing this. It will come up with all different ways to make you feel uncomfortable trying to encourage you to halt the mission for change, to turn back because stuck is safe. The inner critic will try tactics of guilt and shame, *"Don't be ungrateful for what you have – others are much worse off, you should think yourself lucky"*, the mean girl tactic, *"Who are you to think you can have more"*, the distraction tactic, *"Wouldn't you be more comfortable watching that new series, this feels like hard work"*, the general critic, *you know this never works"*, and then there is the one that gets us all to doubt not just whether our dreams are possible but whether we are deserving individuals, *"you are not good enough"*.

In Chapter Three, we will delve further into the inner critic so for now, just try and observe what the inner critic is saying. Have you ever subjected yourself to questioning whether you are normal? Is it normal to want more? Is it normal to think the way I do? Is it normal to react the way I do? Clients are often fearful to raise the question as to whether they are normal just in case by saying it out loud, the whole universe will find out they are different.

Normal. What is normal? And who wants to be normal, anyway? Any quest to be normal should be abandoned right now! It's not a quest for normal, well, not if you are looking for something beyond survival. This is a quest for happya and that will be dependent on you embracing your unique self.

A consensus of "normal", doesn't mean it's right or the only way. It simply means several people have the same opinion and let's be clear that's only based on the people whose opinion has been heard. Here's the thing, there are over eight billion people in the world, and I guarantee you haven't surveyed all of them! Think about it, if only 1% of people agreed with you that would still be 80 million people!

Your sense of normal is part of those beliefs, most of which are installed into you by the age of seven years old and are very much subject to your environment, the influences on your life and your experiences. Is it normal to feel the way you do? Is it normal to think the way you do? Is it normal to behave the way you do? YES! It is *your* normal. It is normal to think, feel, behave, react and respond the way you do, given the unique person you are. Do you think, feel, behave, react and respond along with the masses? Do you follow the consensus? Maybe, but maybe not! Now, here is a decision you need to make, do you want to be hidden in the consensus? Or are you really searching for acceptance to be the individual you are?

As a human, you have free will, the capacity to make choices and decisions that are not determined by a predisposed code. You have the freedom to shape and express yourself based on your own preferences and choices. You are free to deviate from the expected norms and that's what makes the world more diverse and colourful. Naturally, to every action, or inaction, there is a corresponding result, but this is the case whether those actions are within the expected norms or not. It is a matter of choice and free will as to whether you want to invite those results.

Free will means that, as humans, we aren't meant to be clones of one another. Yet what compromises our willingness to embrace our uniqueness is our innate need to survive. That need for survival implores us to be a part of a community because isolation or being a lone wolf is not safe. As with everything in life, it's a fine balance that needs to be struck.

So, when you next find yourself questioning whether it is "*normal*" to think, feel, or behave a certain way, or perhaps when others are challenging you for doing something different, ask yourself the following:

Are you someone who is inspired by words like compliant, plain, conforming, accommodating, pliable, obedient, and docile? Or are you someone who wants to be an individual, following your own path, standing up for your beliefs, setting your own standards, feeling heard, and living life how you want it to be? The journey to finding your happya is about feeling inspired, joyful, motivated and driven. These things can only be found if you are willing to show up for who you really are and make the changes in your life to support you on that journey to live your life in alignment and celebrate your individuality. You do this by truly listening to yourself.

It isn't going to be easy; I know you have already tried different books and resources and you may be asking yourself, well what's different this time? Well, my friend, the power is within you. What it takes is for you to fully commit to the process, invest in yourself and gather the support and accountability to help you along the way. Happya is just a part of the process.

It can be challenging as it's akin to playing yourself and your opponent in your own mind. You are opening yourself to be vulnerable, giving yourself the self-love and compassion you need, all whilst challenging yourself to do things differently. You must acknowledge that making this change is going to be tough and it will take time. It can be done, but don't punish yourself for needing help along the way. Accepting support and recognising your needs not only enables growth but also energises you and opens you up to new opportunities.

So, let's embrace your uniqueness, normalise your struggles, challenge the judgement, develop self-compassion, remove the mask hiding who you really are and accept you. As outlined, this isn't a quick fix. The purpose of this book is not to simply treat the symptoms and give you some inspiring statements which quickly fade. Appeasing you with superficial strategies in the long term will result in you, once again, feeling lost and stuck and further questioning your ability to change. Happya is not a superficial approach that will leave you feeling like a failure when it doesn't work. There's a reason the quick wins fade as quickly as they started, it's because they fail to address the root cause. They simply relieve a symptom and when the underlying issue is left untreated it gets worse. If you don't listen to your inner self and to the issues it is facing, like a petulant child, it will simply shout louder.

Embracing your uniqueness is a powerful step towards understanding and accepting your authentic self. Take some time to think about all the things that make you exceptional. Include your strengths, character traits, passions and accomplishments. Then, equally important, is to embrace the parts you consider less than exceptional because they also play a role in who you are. The collaboration of your strengths and vulnerabilities is what makes you whole. It is time to let go of the myth that we must strive for perfection and to be good at all things, nobody has it all figured out. It is time to celebrate everything that is a part of who you are.

Remember, there are additional bonus resources available to you to help support you along your journey, www.happyacoach.com/bloomingbonus.

If you find yourself feeling overwhelmed, anxious, or uncertain then be assured it is a natural part of the process and life. If it gets too much, allow yourself some time and space to reflect and show yourself some compassion. In the next chapter, we will be covering practices to help you with managing uncertainty. Often, what will be coming up here is a comparison with others. However, what you are comparing is a highly edited version of one person with the detailed and insightful version you have yourself. The only way this is going to serve you is to increase feelings of inadequacy.

It isn't just social media where people give a certain view of their lives, it is in every interaction. Think of how often in a day you speak with someone, and you edit your true feelings and responses to give them an offering of something that is considered acceptable. Obviously, there are times when your energy is either low or supercharged, your emotions run away with you, and you say more than you intended to disclose, or behave in a way that, on reflection, you'd have chosen not to. Don't worry, emotions will be covered in more detail in Chapter Five. The point is you only ever see what another person wants you to. So, when you consider how much of yourself and your inner thoughts you share, you can be assured the people around you are doing the same. You can guarantee you are not alone in your way of thinking; it's just others aren't sharing.

Remember, trust yourself and start to listen to that inner wisdom that has always been there. It's time to start listening to yourself and to start showing up as who you really are. Yes, it's going to be uncomfortable a while longer but be assured, as feelings of self-worth increase and you establish healthy boundaries, the social comparisons that are challenging you right now will start to fade.

With these thoughts in mind, go and take a look at yourself in the mirror. Give yourself the time and space to do this when you won't be disturbed or distracted. It doesn't need to be long. What do you see in the mirror? Who is that person? What does the person looking back at you need from you? How do they feel? What do they want from life? Are they where they want to be?

If you find the inner critic coming up, tell them this is not their time to speak, that this is a moment for you to be kind to yourself and to observe the reflection looking back at you without judgement. Look beyond the surface-level judgement of how youthful your skin looks, how styled your hair is, or how you have aged. Look beyond the outer packaging. What do you see beneath the surface? Let's start the process of unveiling your true self, the opinions you hold of yourself. It is time to face who you really are in that mirror and get comfortable with who you are.

The person you see looking back at you has endured a challenging journey. They have experienced both highs and lows.

They have had to face the darkness, but they have also been guided by the light. They yearn for something more. They yearn for a different way of living. They yearn to be heard and accepted for who they really are.

It is in your power to give them all that they need. Now is the time to make them a promise, a promise that you will not leave them, that you have got this now and you are going to love and support them going forward. Yes, you are going to face challenges, but you have access to the resources you need to make a difference. Perhaps you need to forgive yourself for not being able to give yourself what you needed in the past but that doesn't need to be the case going forward.

Now is the time to make a commitment to yourself. This is your time to make everything you dreamed of happen. If you truly want change, if you are ready to commit to taking action, to do things differently, and to step into your power, it is going to require you to commit to the process. It is going to require you to make a commitment to yourself. Even if the vision is not yet clear and you have no idea what needs to be done, the commitment you make is one to yourself to never leave who you are behind again. The promise is that you will love and care for yourself and will fight for your right to be heard.

To ensure you keep yourself accountable, write your commitment down and sign it. Keep this just for yourself or if you are willing, share your commitment on your social media, or if you'd feel safer, share with the happya community using the #Iamhappya and tag me too. Include in your commitment why you are doing this and why you want to make a change - Why you deserve to find your happya. Make a commitment to how you are going to show up and the priority you are going to give to the process. Include in your commitment how you will approach challenges and overcome barriers.

When you have done this, congratulate yourself for taking this step. Acknowledge your emotions and recognise that today is the first day of your next chapter. Your commitment is going to be there to support you along the way and will help focus your mind and actions when things get uncomfortable and when you are feeling a little challenged. Having acknowledged that this journey is going to be challenging and deciding to continue to do it anyway, it's important that you prepare yourself to ensure that not only are you successful in navigating your way towards a happya life, but you can also support yourself and maintain your wellbeing in the longer term. In the next chapter, you will be introduced to the Happya Survival Kit. Remember, take your time and allow yourself the space to process the information that is presented. Connect with that person you saw in the mirror daily, check in with them to find out how they are doing and how they need to be heard. It may take some time to fully hear their voice because they have been censored or perhaps even silenced for some time. As you begin to peel back the layers, their voice will become clearer and will blend with how you are showing up in life, to become one.

When you are ready, let's start the next chapter and ensure you have the support you need to feel your best and nurture your inner self so you can grow, flourish, thrive and become blooming happya.

"Self-care is giving the world the best of you, instead of what's left of you."

— KATIE REED

CHAPTER 2

THE HAPPYA SURVIVAL KIT

As you are introduced to the Happya Survival Kit, let's first delve into the concept of "happya", the elusive search for happiness, what it really means, and how it aligns with your overall well-being. First, let's extract the nuances between the feeling of joy and elation from an overall sense of well-being. These, whilst intertwined, are two separate entities and yet often collectively referred to as happiness.

Sometimes you will refer to happiness in relation to your feelings of joy - an emotion that provides an immediate sense of excitement, delight, and euphoria, and hopefully, something you get to experience regularly. But what brings you joy? Is it a surprise? An adventure? Travel? Comedy? Hobbies? Entertaining? Socialising? Joy can be found in anything from anthropology to zoology, but whatever it is that brings you joy, this feeling will be relatively short-lived. Have you ever heard the phrase "too much of a good thing"? Excessive amounts of joy would be unnatural and exhausting as the body is flooded with natural opiates. However, whilst joy itself may be fleeting, as with everything, it evokes a chain reaction of physiological and psychological reactions which play a part in your happiness, also referred to as your well-being. Whilst joy is an emotion, your well-being is a state. Even in the most difficult times, when your well-being is challenged and life feels difficult, there can be moments of joy.

When using happiness to refer to your overall well-being, it refers to a state extending way beyond your physical health. Happiness is about feeling good and functioning well, characterised by feelings of fulfilment and contentment. It's about achieving a sense of inner harmony and balance, where your passions, needs and wants are in alignment with your daily life and where you can experience feelings of joy and excitement alongside peace, calm and clarity. It provides you with a sense of safety and control, a feeling of achievement and fulfilment. Whilst positive emotions contribute to your well-being, negative emotions and challenges can detract. That said, negative emotions have an important role to play in your life. This will be covered further in Chapter Five. As with everything in life, it's about maintaining a fine balance, and navigating your personal growth whilst experiencing the highs and lows that life offers.

The components underpinning your well-being cater to both your physical and mental needs. These include your nutrition, a feeling of safety and belonging, and a healthy sense of self. All these elements demand continuous and ongoing self-care. Just as you nurture your body, you must care for your mind and spirit but the formula for your well-being is yours alone, influenced by your unique self and the circumstances and surroundings you find yourself in. Happiness is not a destination, it can't be found in material possessions, even though they may bring you joy, neither is it a one-time achievement.

As we explore the concept of well-being further, it is useful to summarise and highlight the common misconceptions about your well-being. Addressing them will pave the way for achieving a positive state of well-being. One common misconception is that positive well-being requires a constant state of emotional happiness (joy), however, your emotional well-being is a fluctuating emotional state intertwined with moments of joy, sadness, anger, and frustration. The highs are just as significant as the lows; a useful analogy may be to consider it as though you can only truly appreciate the light when you've experienced the darkness.

Next, is the belief that happiness is determined by external factors such as wealth, success, relationships, or environment. Whilst these can contribute, internal factors such as mindset and gratitude provide a more significant role in shaping your well-being. Others believe being happy requires an absence of negative emotions and may even avoid challenges, risks or difficult emotions. However, positive psychology demonstrates the presence of negative emotions is essential to personal growth and resilience. From every experience you encounter, there are lessons to be learned and wisdom to behold. Well-being is also not a destination at which you will arrive. It is in the pursuit of meaningful goals and living authentically, with a healthy, balanced perspective and ego. There is no secret formula and is unique to you. It is not selfish to pursue your own well-being, it is contagious and causes a ripple effect in other people's lives. People with a positive state of well-being are more compassionate, generous and supportive.

Perhaps now is the time to discuss the topic of your ego because it is often misrepresented and, along with the inner critic, treated quite harshly. The thing is your ego is extremely important, essential in fact. Ego is often labelled as arrogance, associated with being over-confident, selfish, negative and fixed with a lack of consideration for others and obviously, for those with an extremely over-inflated ego, that may be the case. However, your ego is essential for your self-identity. It allows you to be your unique self, recognising your own needs and desires. It helps you strike the right balance between only serving your own needs and consideration of societal expectations. It also helps you adapt to your environment, make informed decisions and assess situations objectively, enabling problem-solving and personal growth. Your ego plays an essential role in developing and maintaining your self-esteem. In essence, your ego is a fundamental part of your psychology to help you navigate life, embrace your individuality and adapt to your surroundings.

By exploring your well-being, not only can you enhance your energy, but you will also begin to uncover the essence of living a "happya" life. Your well-being and your vision of a happya life are a dynamic duo, inextricably linked. Happya is your unique recipe for living in alignment with your true self. Accomplishing your happya is to achieve a sense of contentment, where clarity, purpose, fulfilment and joy all intertwine to create a sense of well-being. It is in the pages of this book that you will be guided to explore your unique recipe, enabling you to release yourself from past trauma and live in a state of survival. There is no shortcut to this discovery, the journey is integral to the process, so enjoy the ride.

Your well-being demands care and attention, your energy must be renewed and replenished. It requires showing yourself self-care, love, empathy and compassion. Having empathy for yourself is about being understanding, kind and respectful towards your own feelings, experiences and struggles. It's about acknowledging your own pain, fears and challenges, without judgement. Compassion takes it a step further, putting empathy into action. It's the moment when you say to yourself, *"I'm going to help you overcome this. I am going to give myself the love and nurturing that I need."* This concept can feel quite uncomfortable if you have been living a life stuck in survival mode where you are just doing everything to get through the day, focusing on other's needs and ignoring your own.

This is where your Happya Survival Kit is a crucial part of your journey. It serves as your ultimate support system for renewing, replenishing, and reviving every facet of your well-being, including your physical, mental, social, and emotional energy. Your Happya Survival Kit is a necessity for everyday life, an integral part of your self-maintenance system ensuring your mind and body run smoothly. Its significance amplifies when you embark on a transformative journey like the one in hand.

No doubt there have already been times in reading this book when you will have felt uncomfortable and there is going to be more of that to come because if you are looking to find your happya, a recipe that has eluded you for some time, there is going to need to be some change. Change will spark fear, and at times, you will become drained from emotional processing. In fact, I often describe the beginning of this journey to be much like running into a burning building - nobody wants to do it but there is a version of yourself in that building that has been left behind and needs you to rescue them so they can be seen and heard. Reconnecting with your authentic self will enable you to live a life filled with meaning and purpose. So, before venturing into that burning building, let's ensure you're properly equipped. Think of your survival kit as your maintenance system. It's all about self-care.

In a world that prioritises performance and success is measured by "doing", the concept of self-care and self-love can feel elusive and self-indulgent, yet it is not a luxury but a necessity, a fundamental part of your life. In this chapter, we explore what you should include in your Happya Survival Kit to support your mind, body and spirit in managing your emotions, thoughts and desires whilst navigating towards your happya.

Let's be clear, self-care isn't about taking a candle-lit bubble bath and getting an early night, neither is it booking a spa break. Whilst these activities help calm your nervous system, they provide a temporary fix, perhaps moments of joy. However, unless they are part of a wider regime of self-care, the results will be short-lived. Whilst self-care is often portrayed as a quick, self-indulgent fix, the reality is this approach compounds feelings of not being good enough. When that bubble bath doesn't deliver relief from the lifetime of challenges you have faced, when it doesn't provide you with the eureka moment where your life is suddenly transformed, you are left feeling abandoned, not good enough and hopeless because it didn't work for you.

Self-care is about giving yourself some love, showing yourself compassion, meeting your needs and re-energising your batteries. You are the most precious thing in the world because there is only one of you. Remember, they broke the mould when you were born and you are 100% irreplaceable, so what deserves more of your attention than looking after yourself? A big *NO!* coming your way if you have just said "my kids", "my dog", "my partner", "work" etc. – You know that's not the right answer. We covered this at the beginning – *you must put your oxygen mask on first!*

It's time to fully embrace your self-care and give yourself some unconditional love, affection and nurturing. It's time to recognise your worth and accept yourself for all you are and all you are not. It's time to prioritise your well-being and show yourself some long-overdue compassion. And this isn't one afternoon of pure indulgence, neither is it something that you save for your birthday, this is something you should - strike that - **must** give yourself every day. Whether that's a high five in the morning, a spa day ritual, or spending twenty minutes meditating. Yes, every day! Show yourself the love you so need and deserve, and it will enable you to sparkle... and when you sparkle, so do others.

And yes, I've heard you say, "*I don't have time to do that.*" You should know by now that I'm not someone who tip-toes around, so here's the thing, *yes,* you do have time. You've had time for all the negativity in your life, and now we are going to be banishing that to the past, there'll be time for positive, deliberate action to take up the space so that procrastination and negativity don't. So, let's make some space and do something positive because believe me, a high five in the morning takes a nano-second! Binge-watching Netflix to try and escape your reality takes hours. I'm not saying you must stop doing the binge, sometimes a good Netflix binge is exactly what you need and anyone who tells you otherwise, tell them I said so (after all, I have an ology!).

Let's be clear, the work you are doing throughout this book is challenging and no doubt, it will increase those jelly wobbles, so your Happya Survival Kit, your maintenance and first aid kit for your mind, body and soul is going to be essential. Nurturing a loving relationship with yourself will have a positive impact on every aspect of your life. When you feel loved and nurtured, it empowers you to face challenges, take action and make changes. Importantly, it also helps the wounds of past trauma to heal. Showing yourself self-love improves feelings of self-worth, the key enabler to success. If you believe you are worthy of your dreams, the probability of you achieving them is exponentially higher. Neuroscience has shown that showing yourself compassion increases brain activity, therefore increasing your mental capacity. Importantly, how you treat yourself is aligned with how you allow others to treat you.

In your pursuit of a happya life, it's imperative to prioritise your well-being and ensure your mind, body and soul are operating efficiently and effectively. To accomplish this, it's essential to recognise that you require a continuous supply of energy. What is crucial to understand is that not all activities, mental or physical, require the same source of energy. Each activity taps into a different source. Think of it as having a different battery pack depending on the type of activity you are engaged in or the challenge you are overcoming. To enhance your ability to thrive in all aspects of your life, you need to restore and renew the energy in each of your battery packs - borrowing energy from other sources of energy leads to burnout and your well-being being compromised. It's also not just about replenishing the energy in your battery pack. If energy is not used, it can also compromise your well-being.

Here's an example. If you work in an environment which is physically challenging, perhaps you're on your feet all day. That activity will draw energy from your physical energy battery. At the end of a busy day, your physical battery will be depleted. If you undertook the task of journaling about how your feet ache, that isn't going to recharge your physical battery. Instead, you need to soak your feet, massage them, put them up for a rest and recharge your physical energy battery. On the other hand, if you have been working on your computer all day and haven't moved, then going for a walk will release the built-up energy in your physical battery pack and allow your mental battery to recharge.

In creating your Happya Survival Kit, it's essential to consider the different types of energy and how you can best replenish and renew each of your battery packs to ensure optimal usage for your happya life. For some of you, your happya life will require a significant physical battery pack, whilst for others, it may be that your emotional battery pack needs more focus. Don't forget, if the energy remains unused, then it will negatively impact other areas. In essence, not only will you need to give yourself a boost in particular areas, but you will also need to put all the battery packs on charge to renew your energy – sleep is a perfect charge for all areas.

The following outlines the different pillars that come together to create your overall well-being. These pillars include physical, emotional, mental, and social energy. For each of these pillars, consider how you will charge your battery pack. Let's look at each and see how you can manage your overall well-being to ensure balance. Remember, you have access to some bonus resources to support you in developing your Happya Survival

Kit, sign up, www.happyacoach.com/bloomingbonus to have these resources delivered straight to your inbox.

Okay, so what do we mean by physical energy? How is your physical energy currently being used? Are you exerting too much or too little? Are you moving regularly, exercising, or challenging yourself physically? Are you getting enough sleep? Are you eating healthy? Are there any pressures impacting your physical well-being now? After reflecting on how you use your physical energy, consider what level of self-care needs to be attributed to attending to your physical self-care needs.

Physical self-care is about engaging in activities such as regular exercise and eating well and balanced nutrition. It includes getting quality sleep and adequate rest, as well as hygiene. These actions not only support your body but also have a positive impact on your mental and emotional well-being. A healthy sleep regime is not just how much sleep but also includes, a calming bedtime routine, ensuring a comfortable sleeping environment and a regular sleeping schedule.

Here are just a few ways in which you can enhance your physical well-being, supporting you towards living a fulfilling life.

Research has shown that spending time outdoors and being in nature holds a plethora of benefits; it reduces stress, improves mood and enhances your immune function. Taking a stroll through a forest, park or any green space can help restore your energy and well-being. Whilst spending time in nature, be mindful of the sights, sounds and sensations around you.

Engaging in activities like yoga and tai chi promotes a connection between your mind and body. These practices have been shown to reduce anxiety and improve overall flexibility and fitness. They provide a sense of balance and tranquillity beyond the session.

Laughter yoga is a practice that combines playful exercises with laughter and scientific research indicates that laughter triggers the release of endorphins, your body's natural feel-good chemicals. This reduces stress, improves cardiovascular health and enhances your immune system.

Take a moment to think about your physical well-being and self-care. How well are you taking care of your physical needs? Are there ways in which you could improve? Contemplate on a scale of 0-10 how charged is your physical energy, with 10 being fully charged and 0 being I have nothing left to give. Think about how you recharge your physical energy daily and then perhaps consider how you can give yourself a boost. For example, maybe you focus on how much water you drink daily and eating healthy, and once a month, you treat yourself to a massage. Remember self-care is not just about the treats and giving yourself a boost but encompasses your regular maintenance. This is a good place to begin when thinking about establishing new habits.

Next, consider your emotional self-care, acknowledging and processing your emotions in healthy ways is a significant part of your well-being. Activities such as practising mindfulness gratitude, undertaking meditation and journaling all support our system to maintain emotional balance. Again, consider how charged your emotional battery is, how well have you been looking after your emotional well-being? What would your score be? Take some time with this and be honest with yourself, and if you know this is an area you struggle with, I want you to pay even closer attention to how you are using your energy. Don't forget to check out the additional resources to support you with this chapter.

Emotional awareness is the practice of recognising, accepting and honouring your feelings without judgement. Acknowledging your feelings and allowing them the space to be heard enables you to process them accordingly, rather than finding yourself acting upon them. Mindfulness exercises can help in observing your emotions as they arise rather than trying to suppress or amplify them.

Engaging in hobbies, interests or creative pursuits that resonate with your passion will bring moments of positivity and satisfaction. They can provide feelings of joy, accomplishment and connection, enhancing your mood and emotional well-being.

Allowing yourself to express and release emotions is liberating and replenishes and enhances your emotional well-being, enabling healing from emotional distress. Activities such as reflective journaling, creative art, or music all enable you to connect with your emotions.

Again, contemplate on a scale of 0-10 how charged is your emotional energy, with 10 being fully charged and 0 being I have nothing left to give. Think about how you recharge your emotional energy daily and consider the different scenarios where your emotional energy feels particularly drained. You may want to consider whether some uses of your emotional energy are even worth it. Are you putting yourself in situations that negatively impact your emotional well-being that you can remove from your life? Perhaps there are individuals who have a detrimental impact on your well-being, and you may want to consider upholding your boundaries. This topic will be covered in Chapter Six.

The third pillar is your mental self-care and involves nurturing and maintaining the health of your cognitive functioning using practices focused on ensuring mental clarity. Activities such as reading, solving puzzles, critical thinking exercises, or learning new skills help keep your mind actively engaged. Your mental energy is consumed by all those problem-solving tasks, decision-making, mental processing, and so much more. If you are doing a lot of this daily, then, to improve your well-being, you need to call time on mental activities and allow yourself time to recharge.

Engagement in activities that challenge and stimulate your mind, resulting in cognitive engagement, enhances your brain's functioning and its neural plasticity. These activities contribute to improved memory, focus and cognitive performance. By embracing these activities, you are giving yourself the mental nourishment needed to thrive.

Cognitive resilience forms another component of your mental self-care. Engaging in positive self-talk helps cultivate an improved state of mental well-being. It's important to pay attention to your inner dialogue and consciously reframe thoughts to challenge limiting beliefs with affirming and empowering thoughts. Cognitive resilience enables you to recover from challenges and setbacks, equipping you to navigate adversity.

Once more, reflect on a scale of 0 to 10 the vitality of your social energy, where 10 represents being fully charged, and 0 signifies complete depletion. Examine how you engage with and replenish your social energy, considering all facets of your life.

The final pillar is social self-care. Consider your social connections, the relationships you have in your life and how you can uphold healthy boundaries. Talking things through with a trusted friend or loved one helps validate and process emotions and gives you a sense of safety and security knowing someone else is there for you.

Social endeavours and interactions such as team sports, dancing and group fitness classes facilitate social bonding. Connecting with others who have similar interests enhances motivation and confidence leading to a more fulfilling life. Whilst some of you may consider yourselves to be introverts this does not preclude the need for social interaction. If you experience social anxiety, this pillar may require you to give yourself additional support, perhaps engaging with others on a one-to-one basis initially.

Your Happya Survival Kit needs to contain elements which support you in each of these areas. Regularly practicing self-care is a priority and if you find it hard to implement, it's time to deliberately schedule the time into your day. Allow it to become part of your morning and bedtime routine. Perhaps you have time in your day when others aren't around that you can call timeout and indulge yourself.

Now you have a clearer understanding of the different pillars of self-care, reflect on how balanced they are. Perhaps notice where there are needs currently unmet. Perhaps you have not previously considered all these different aspects of well-being. Having identified all these it's time to think about how you can make this a focus in your life. You are going to need to start putting them into your schedule in permanent marker. There is always time to be found when sufficient priority is given, and you have full permission to erase procrastination from the schedule and put your needs first.

It's also beneficial to put together a list of things that give you an instant boost when times are hard - your emergency Happya Survival Kit. Having this list prepared makes it easier to support yourself when you are not feeling your best. Think of what comforts you, recharges you and brings you joy. It really doesn't matter what it is but being aware of the different ways in which you can support yourself can help identify the need that isn't being met. Spending time meditating and journaling is not going to improve your well-being if you are craving social inter-action and vice versa. Some suggestions for this emergency list are included in the bonus materials. Some examples from clients include a manicure, flowers, reading, a specific chocolate bar, calling a particular friend, or a particular song to change your mood.

Being intentional about managing your self-care regime is not selfish, there is no guilt allowed for giving yourself what you need as, ultimately, by doing this, you are able to effectively care for others. Self-care provides a connection with your own wants and needs, improving self-worth. It also helps to prevent stress and burnout and conversely, helps with productivity. As you practice self-care, you will begin to foster a deep sense of self-love and appreciation, embracing your unique self, which supports you in living authentically. Doubling down on self-care whilst you embark on this journey of personal growth and discovery is even more important. As you own up to your vulnerabilities and make changes in your life, it can increase feelings of fear and anxiety. Being uncomfortable is not something to avoid but a sign that change is coming and to support your nervous system in understanding that change is a positive requires you to show yourself love and compassion.

Check out www.happyacoach.com/survivalkit to find additional resources to support you in putting together your Survival Kit.

As you continue this journey of change and take yourself and your life beyond survival towards finding your happya, you will uncover a greater sense of awareness of who you are and what your needs are. Throughout the journey, ensure you have your Happya Survival Kit to hand so you can ensure your well-being is maintained, giving you the boost you need. As you delve deeper, make sure you make the necessary adjustments.

"Your past is not the end of your story; you get to write the next chapter."

— UNKNOWN

CHAPTER 3

NARRATING YOUR JOURNEY

N ow you have your Happya Survival Kit to support you, it's time for you to reflect on your personal narrative and resilience. As you navigate your way to finding your happya it is essential to reflect and appreciate the path that has brought you here. In undertaking this approach, not only will it improve your self-awareness, but it will also start to sow the seeds of transformation.

Your personal narrative is the story of your life, the moments that have defined you, the challenges that have tested you and the triumphs that have uplifted you. It's a narrative filled with resilience, strength and untapped potential. Your journey towards self-discovery is an act of self-compassion, a practice deeply rooted in the happya philosophy. By embracing your narrative, you're not only recognising your past, but you're also setting your course for a future that resonates with authenticity, purpose and joy. It is not just about the physical journey you have travelled, where you have lived, places you have been and sights you have seen, but equally, it is about understanding your inner journey. It's about navigating your thoughts, emotions and beliefs.

In the following chapter, we'll explore what it means to be the author of your own story and how understanding your past can empower you to create a future that aligns with your true self. Whilst we cannot always control the things that happen to us, we can control how we respond to them. By understanding the chapters of our past, we can learn and grow, taking that wisdom to enable us to achieve growth and achieve a happya life.

You are encouraged to approach this chapter with an open heart and a curious mind. Your story is like no other, it is as unique as you and whilst you may be tempted to make comparisons to others remember, from the moment you are conceived, you are your own unique self and are subject to your own set of experiences. Whilst your experiences may appear aligned with someone else, they do not stand in your shoes, they have not walked your path and they do not have the unique identity that we celebrate as being you. Let's explore the chapters of your life through a lens of self-compassion and understanding and uncover the power within your narrative and the resilience that will guide you towards a truly happya life.

Positive psychology has demonstrated that those who embrace their life story, including adversity, tend to achieve higher levels of life satisfaction. The act of recognising and accepting your journey can prove liberating, allowing you to free yourself from the weight of regret, blame and guilt, and create space for healing and personal growth. Embracing your life's journey builds resilience - your ability to bounce back from adversity. Resilience is not just an innate skill but can be developed, supporting you in navigating future challenges leading to a brighter future.

Now, for some of you, the thought of reflecting on the past is going to be challenging and you may need to get some professional one-on-one support. However, if you feel your past is something you can navigate without compromising your mental well-being, I still urge you to think about how you will recharge your emotional energy from your Happya Survival Kit. Everyone has experience of trauma and it's essential to show yourself compassion. Reflecting on the past chapters of your life will inevitably bring up a range of emotions and in doing so, it's important to show yourself love, understanding and recognition for all you have endured and all you have achieved.

Before we delve deeper into your journey, it's important to understand what is and isn't trauma. Trauma isn't about the sensational headlines and horror stories fed to you by the media and entertainment industry. Trauma can arise from seemingly minor events in your childhood to the major events that invade your life. The biggest misunderstanding around trauma is that trauma is not the event but the aftermath of the event, the damage an event or circumstance does. Trauma is the impact an event has on your physiological and psychological well-being. It's irrelevant whether the event was earth-shattering or a pothole in the road of life. What matters is its effect. It's essential to acknowledge that your experience, your story and your trauma are valid, size doesn't matter! Whilst the magnitude of the event itself will have a correlation to the damage caused, it is also true that the most seemingly insignificant event can still do significant damage to you and your well-being. Think about the time someone made a seemingly insignificant comment to you and yet it cut deep.

There is no trauma Olympics or hierarchy of suffering. Everyone's experiences are unique, and the emotional impact on an individual is personal. What's important is to acknowledge the impact events have on you and your life's narrative. Trauma is often a misunderstood concept and a label most people do not want to own. Perhaps some of you don't feel good enough to accept your experience of trauma, perhaps your inner dialogue is telling you how it wasn't that bad or could have been worse. A response heard from domestic abuse survivors, those who have been widowed, or experienced a serious injury through an accident is a feeling of expected gratitude that it wasn't worse - *He hasn't hit me that hard. I'm lucky I didn't die.* People often come to me saying how guilty they feel that their traumatic experience doesn't equate to what I have experienced and in turn, I have caught myself doing the same. You do not need to justify why you feel the way you do but acknowledge the fact that it is how you feel and that you deserve compassion. Your thoughts and feelings are your mind and body's way of keeping you safe - it's just sometimes messages get muddled, misinterpreted, or perhaps there is information missing.

Whether you reject the term trauma or not, it's beneficial to understand what it entails. Trauma occurs when you are exposed to distressing events or a series of events that overwhelm your ability to cope. It can result from various experiences, whether it's on the top ten list of stressful events or not. It can stem from stressors such as illness or living in an unsafe environment. It can result from not having your needs met, your sense of safety being undermined, or your well-being challenged. The consequences of trauma do not just affect your mind but can have a profound impact on your physical and emotional well-being. It can disrupt your future sense of safety and trust, leaving you feeling vulnerable. As already mentioned, trauma is not the event itself, but the aftermath of damage caused and if not processed and released, it can impact other aspects of your life and continue to impact your future life's journey. It can affect relationships, work, personal growth and achievement as well as negatively impact your overall well-being and satisfaction with life.

The impact of trauma can leave you feeling drained of both emotional and psychological energy, leaving you limited in your capacity to manage daily life. This exhaustion can manifest as physical symptoms, having a profound effect on your life. Chapter Seven will focus more on how to process and release the impact of trauma. In this chapter, we are seeking to acknowledge the psychological wounds of trauma before we are ready to let go. Positive psychology research has demonstrated that individuals who confront and process traumatic experiences are more likely to experience post-traumatic growth.

Post-traumatic growth is the concept that in the aftermath of trauma, you may not only recover but also experience personal growth and positive changes in life. The long-term consequences of experiencing a traumatic event are not restricted to a life of survival but can extend far beyond, where you take the experience to achieve greater satisfaction in life and enhance your well-being. Within the experience of a traumatic event is the opportunity to grow, flourish and thrive. Experiencing trauma can often provide a new perspective on life, providing a greater appreciation for life and gaining a greater sense of meaning and purpose. It can lead to enhanced emotional resilience, making you better equipped to handle future stress and adversity. Your efforts to foster stronger and more meaningful relationships with others grow, as does your capacity for compassion and empathy. It offers the potential for you to empower yourself to say, "*Not today universe, I'm not going to let this beat me*", and it is in recognising your potential and the possibility that the motivation, the belief that you deserve more and your capability for success lies, and happiness is within reach. Chapter Four will cover mindset and your potential in far greater detail. It isn't that post-traumatic growth can negate the pain and distress caused by trauma, but rather it represents the potential for positive change to emerge. When your belief system and life are significantly destabilised, it offers the opportunity to rebuild with the wisdom that you now have. Think of it as if your twenty-year-old self knew what you do today, what decisions would they have made? What would have been important to you that you didn't realise would matter so much at the time? Also, think about that version of yourself and what their hopes and dreams were because this will help you to connect with the authentic version of yourself before you became weighed with the beliefs of society.

Recognising trauma's impact on you empowers you to take control of your narrative. Your journey to happya is not about erasing or ignoring the past chapters of your life but transforming them into sources of strength and wisdom. It's about understanding how you have got to where you are and meeting your needs to get you ready for the next chapter of your life.

There is a big distinction between happya and the historic approaches of the mental health system, and that is how trauma is processed. Traditional counselling and techniques, such as cognitive behavioural therapy, have been immensely valuable, however, as scientific knowledge and understanding have grown, there is an increased awareness that for some, these may inadvertently reinforce trauma and cause people to find themselves stuck. This is particularly true when dwelling on past traumatic experiences. For some, it can cause trauma re-enactment, where survivors find themselves retelling their trauma without processing and achieving relief or resolution. In essence, revisiting the trauma embeds it further into their psyche, making it an ongoing part of their story.

More recent research in neuroscience has shown that trauma can alter brain structures and their functionality, particularly in relation to emotional regulation and the processing of memories. When people continually revisit trauma without proper support, it can reinforce the neural pathways associated with fear, anxiety and distress, and can remain stuck. At happya, the focus is centred on your well-being, taking a positive approach to recovery that is trauma-informed, so you don't get stuck.

When revisiting past chapters of your life it is essential to first establish a sense of safety and that you are supported, hence the relevance of your Happya Survival Kit. If you have a significant history of trauma, then this activity is certainly something that should be done with the support of a qualified therapist. It's also relevant here to note that you shouldn't wait until you can't cope before you seek help - you, your mind and body need regular check-ups. Just like having your car serviced, you need to ensure your engine is running smoothly. This is a key learning point from my own journey. If only I had given myself permission to seek the help I needed a decade earlier, I could have benefited from the wisdom it gave me sooner. I didn't need to wait for the permission given to me by others when my husband passed away, I deserved the love and compassion way before that!

At happya, you are encouraged to fill your survival kit with tools to help you cope with trauma-related distress, relaxation techniques such as breath work, meditation, mindfulness and various self-soothing strategies. Taking notice of the bodily sensations and emotions related to the turmoil you experience helps process trauma on a somatic level. On this journey, you are not revisiting the past to come to some form of acceptance but to learn and heal from it. To understand its lessons and to grow so that you allow yourself to bloom happya. In essence, the past is not a place to set up camp but a place to harvest the learning and move on.

Let's begin to explore your life's narrative. Imagine your life as a journey and along the way you have been collecting experiences, some of them are light whilst others are heavy. All these experiences have been loaded into a backpack that you carry with you. In positive psychology, the backpack is seen not only as a burden but also as a resource of strength and resilience. Every experience you have encountered offers a source of wisdom, and research has shown those who view their life experiences as valuable lessons tend to experience higher levels of well-being and life satisfaction. Exploring the contents of your backpack and proactively determining the things you wish to carry into your next chapter enables you to start to identify what is truly of value to you and your happya, and what you can let go of, releasing yourself from the burden of carrying unnecessary baggage.

Take some time now to consider the contents of your own life's backpack. What experiences have you carried with you throughout your journey? Think about the times when you faced adversity, when you felt you just had no more to give but you carried on regardless. These moments are a testament to the strength and resilience within. What have these challenges taught you? It is often in these moments you can discover the most important life lessons. In Chapter Seven, we will be delving into this topic further but it's worthwhile starting to gain that insight here.

But your life's journey is not solely defined by challenge and adversity. It will also be adorned with moments of joy and success. Consider the times when you achieved your goals, both big and small – remember, size doesn't matter, we are talking about the impact it has on you, not anyone else's perception or experience. Give your ego the nourishment it deserves by acknowledging you for all you have achieved. Recall the experiences that filled your heart with joy and satisfaction. Celebrate your accomplishments and acknowledge your achievements, recognising where you have gone way beyond the expectations you or others had in your own ability and potential.

Acknowledging your achievements will support you in cultivating a positive outlook, whilst savouring them will further motivate you to continue your journey and provide evidence of your abilities to succeed. Success is a testament to your determination and capabilities. No person's life is solely determined by challenges and adversity. Recognising and celebrating your achievements plays a pivotal role in leading a fulfilling life and it might just surprise you how much you have to be proud of. Celebrating you and your success is not egotistical or arrogant but is about embracing your true potential. Remember, whilst the ego often is portrayed as being the source of negativity it is an essential part of your survival and well-being. Your ego serves as the interface between your internal dialogue and the external world. It is a fundamental aspect of you. Psychologically, your ego identifies you with distinct thoughts, feelings and experiences, helping you establish boundaries, make decisions and interact with the world. Consider the ego as the captain of your ship, navigating you through the waters of your life. It's the foundation of you and differentiates you from every other person in the world. If left unchecked, it can lead to negative behaviours such as arrogance and selfishness however, it also needs love and nurture. In the next chapter, we will be exploring your identity further.

When you take charge of your own life's narrative, you become the author of your own story. You gain the power to reframe and reinterpret your experiences. What may, on the surface, be seen as setbacks can become the stepping stones to transformation and personal growth. Consider the internal narrative you have been telling yourself. How might reframing your narrative lead to a more empowered existence? Remember, you get to decide. It isn't about denying the challenges you've faced or the mistakes you've made. It's about shifting your perspective and finding new meaning in your narrative. You are not defined by your past; you are defined by the narrative you choose to follow in writing your next chapter.

Let's take a moment to recognise your inner critic. That relentless voice that often likes to rise from the depths of within and cast doubt on your ability to self-author your narrative. Contrary to much of the advice out there, rather than trying to banish this voice to some hidden depth of yourself, it is much more effective to gain an understanding of the origins of this inner critic and the role it has played in your past. Your inner critic, despite its uninvited appearances, comes from a place of self-preservation. It is a voice that is there to protect you from perceived threats, both internal and external. The intention is to keep you vigilant of potential threats to your safety. Whilst its aim is to protect you, it often challenges your well-being, sense of worth, capability and belief in your potential. Recognising your inner critic's role and its intentions will enable you to reclaim your narrative. Rather than trying to squeeze it out of existence, if you acknowledge its presence and understand why it feels the need to show up, you take control and can provide the reassurance necessary that you've got this. You get to hold the power. You don't need to succumb to your inner critic but disempower it through self-compassion. If you find you are struggling with your inner critic, check out the bonus resources for some practical strategies for taming your inner critic and don't forget to check in with your Happya Survival Kit.

Now you have explored your past chapters and are committed to taking control of the narrative, an opportunity waits for you to become the narrator of your story. Self-authoring is not about recounting your past; it's about seizing the pen and writing your story in a way that aligns with your true self. This process enables you to move beyond the constraints of the past and presents an opportunity for self-discovery, empowerment and transformation. You have the opportunity and ability to reclaim your story and view your past, present and future through a lens of empowerment and purpose. Along your journey of transformation, this is your opportunity to write your past narrative with a growth mindset, to enable you to build a future on the firm foundation of acknowledging your story. This is your opportunity for your true self to be heard, for you to be acknowledged and, most importantly, accepted.

As the self-author of your past story, you get to tell the story. You are not a passive character in a predetermined plot; you are the author, and you have the power to determine the narrative and make yourself the hero. It's about writing the chapters where you made mistakes not as regrets but as opportunities from which to learn and grow. It's about learning to forgive yourself for mistakes you made when you didn't know better. It's where you can celebrate your achievements with gratitude. The mindset of empowerment is a recurring theme throughout this book, harness its power. It's the acknowledgement that you have control over your future, you are not merely the outcome of a predetermined destiny. The belief that your actions can influence your life's direction is a core tenet of happya-proven scientific research. It is the difference between growth and a state of survival or helplessness.

In the process of self-authoring, you are not rewriting history to deny or dismiss your past. Instead, you present it with a lens of intention and purpose. Your mistakes are mere stepping stones, providing the wisdom to get it right in the next chapter. Your narrative is your legacy. By taking charge of your narrative, you ensure it reflects your true self, your values and your vision for a happya life. Take the time to explore the past chapters of your life and empower yourself with that learning for writing the next.

In this chapter, we have sought to explore your past narrative, the journey that has led you to this significant juncture in your life's story. Through the lens of recognition and acceptance, you can unlock the power to liberate yourself from regret and blame. This has been a journey not only in the acknowledgement of the adversities you've faced but also a celebration of the remarkable achievements you've attained. This dual recognition provides a cornerstone of resilience, empowering you for the journey ahead. This newfound empowerment will serve to enhance your well-being and improve your overall satisfaction with life.

We delved into the realm of trauma, unravelling its significant impact on emotional well-being and the importance of recognising trauma not as an event, but as the impact it leaves on you and your life. We also ventured into the inner critic, that persistent voice within that seeks to safeguard you through critique, but we also unveiled the potential that compassion and understanding can have.

Ultimately, you have the power to craft a story of empowerment, one that magnifies the positive aspects of your experiences and finds growth in adversity and challenge. Your narrative is a powerful tool, and this chapter has prepared you to use it in the most impactful and positive way.

In the chapter ahead, we will focus on uncovering your true self, delving into the essence of your being, and revealing the unique individual you are. It will explore your passions, values and desires, and discover the authentic self that has been buried beneath the needs of others and prioritisation of expectations for so long. It's a journey of self-discovery to enrich your happya life.

"True belonging never asks us to change who we are. True belonging requires us to be who we are."

— BRENE BROWN

CHAPTER 4

HARMONISE YOUR AUTHENTICITY

In this chapter, the aim is to focus you back to the essence of who you really are as we delve into self-discovery to uncover and reconnect with your authentic self. After so many years of putting other's needs ahead of your own, taking a back seat and taking on board the expectations of the world around you, it's easy to understand how your sense of who you really are is difficult to uncover and connect with. In the hustle and bustle of life, it's all too easy to lose sight of the person you once knew well. When you were younger, you had fewer responsibilities and you got to be yourself. Then, as you grow and mature, you hopefully get the opportunity to explore your identity and find what suits you. However, over the years, as you navigate societal expectations, and take on the weight of trauma and the burden of feeling *"not enough"*, you can slowly drift away from your core self. It's a complicated path to follow and you may have had strong opinions around you that influenced you in taking certain paths. Parents, siblings, caregivers, teachers, family, friends and your community all provide a level of expectation. Some will give instruction whilst others will perhaps offer you more space to determine your own path. Some of you will have had to negotiate events and circumstances which we'd all by choice be able to protect a child from. If you grew up in a household where there was a lot of instability - perhaps you took on roles within the family that were beyond your years or maybe your behaviour was shaped by a need to keep yourself safe. But here's the truth: your true self is still there, waiting and wanting to be discovered. In fact, as you continue this path you will begin to hear their voice getting louder from within.

Whatever your story, the journey of your experiences, your guides along the way and your interpretation of these have all added layers to your identity. Some of these layers will enable personal growth whilst others have perhaps served to keep the authentic you safe and hidden. Now, as an adult who has control and influence over your own life, you get to remove those layers and be the person you want to be. This is not as easy as it sounds as you can often take responsibility for performing roles you weren't meant for. Maybe you are someone who has taken control through being planned and organised but naturally finds more joy in chaos. Perhaps you've had to be in control for so long and it's now time to try something different. Whilst in previous chapters of your life it may have felt unsafe not to be planned and organised, it's now time to take control of your life in your own way. You no longer need to live in a way that feels unsafe, you can make your own decisions and access the resources you need to support you.

It's time to start believing in your potential to do anything. Whilst an historic lack of safety, belief or resources to do something different prohibited you in the past from doing things differently, it's time to let go of the ways that weren't yours in the first place. Perhaps you're someone who has found it safer to be strong and uphold barriers and you have been hiding empathy through fear of judgement or lack of self-worth. If it has felt unsafe in the past to be who you really are, then it will take some encouragement to allow those natural traits to resurface, so please be kind to yourself on this journey. It will take time, but you will get there; you just need to show some more compassion and reach into your Happya Survival Kit for support.

So, let's get started. This chapter and this book are not about scratching the surface and implementing some superficial rituals into your life. They're here to enable you to make lasting change and to live intentionally and to do that, *you* must be right at the heart of your happya life. You are the most important ingredient in your happya life. By uncovering and understanding who you are - your values, what holds meaning and purpose for you, and what ignites joy and fulfils your passions - you can build a life and achieve a dream that really matters to you. The journey towards authenticity begins with understanding the core of you. Positive psychology teaches us that the foundation of personal growth and fulfilment begins with your authentic self. Scientific studies have consistently shown that individuals who have a clear sense of their values, interests and identity experience greater satisfaction in life, have an improved level of well-being and are more resilient in the face of adversity.

If you aren't sure where to begin and don't know what you want, don't worry because this chapter and the bonus resources are all here to guide you. You'll learn how to map your values and interests, identify what is important to you, get to grips with your strengths and personality, instil a growth mindset and lay the foundation for a more authentic life. This is not just a philosophical quest; all the techniques suggested are grounded in the principles of positive psychology, supported by scientific findings, and form the foundation of happya.

To embrace your true self is to first understand your identity, what it is, what defines it for you and how the disconnection has developed over the years. Your identity is the experiences, beliefs, values, traits and aspirations you hold that make you uniquely you. In life, your identity is presented in different facets, the roles you are taken on or inherit, whether that's as a daughter, wife, mother, friend, volunteer, professional or any other role. Consider how many different roles you play each day and over the course of a year. Each role contributes to the richness of your life, but the roles must be played as yourself and not to the expectation others hold over that position. To maintain your own identity when representing yourself, you must have clarity over who you really are. This includes understanding your beliefs, both conscious and unconscious, your values, the guiding principles of your identity and life, your life narrative (as explored in Chapter Three) and the passions that ignite your spirit and bring you joy.

Let's first explore and acknowledge the disconnection that may have developed over the years. This acknowledgement is not to pass judgement on yourself or others, but to give compassionate recognition of where you are in your journey and the influences there have been. As already outlined, you've been wearing different hats and playing different roles and amidst these, it's easy to understand how other's needs have been absorbed as your own. Life can be unpredictable and challenging, and trauma can further challenge your sense of self-worth and purpose. It can throw you off course. Societal expectations place pressure on you to conform, providing a list of all the things you *"should"* do. If you were to think about the things on your list for the next week, how many of them are things you *should* do rather than *want* to do? If your emotional state has been challenged, you will have experienced self-doubt and perhaps you have been questioning yourself.

When you consider all of these, it is no wonder you deviated from your intended path. Even the smallest of adjustments makes the biggest difference over time. The ease with which you get distracted is enhanced if you lack a strong vision of what you want at the start of your journey. We will be covering your vision in Chapter Eight, so don't worry, this book is here to support you in providing you with the tools you need so that you don't get lost again. Acknowledging the disconnection with self-compassion is essential along with making the commitment to bridge the gap and get yourself back on course. Connect with that feeling of wanting something more, of going beyond survival. This is how you connect with the strength and power within you. This is the approach for connecting with who you really are, the version of you that is going to support you in achieving your dreams, so it's worthwhile spending time nurturing and getting to know them.

In the pursuit of reconnecting with your authentic self, you will need to engage in a reflective exploration, you will need to be open and honest. Mindfulness is a practice that can help you reconnect with your innermost thoughts and feelings and is a practice you can incorporate into your daily life. It helps you to connect with what is truly important to you. Mindfulness is the technique of being present in the moment without judgement. It's about observing your thoughts, emotions and sensations as they arise, without trying to actively change or suppress them. It could be a tool for you to add to your Happya Survival Kit. It is certainly an approach to undertake ahead of self-reflection. Find a quiet space and give attention to your breath. Focus on the inhale and exhale and notice the sensations. Bring self-awareness into how you are feeling and consider some of the thoughts that have been arising on this journey, without judgement. Write down your thoughts and acknowledge your emotions without judgement. Acceptance of your emotions is at the core of showing self-compassion and we will be delving further into your emotions in the next chapter. The more time you spend practising mindfulness, the greater your ability to connect with your inner self will become and your awareness and appreciation will become increasingly compassionate. Further support on practising mindfulness is included in the bonus resources.

Let's start by exploring your values, often considered the compass of your life. They play a pivotal role in shaping your beliefs and guiding your decisions and they offer a sense of direction. Values are not merely abstract concepts; they are the moral principles that underpin your identity and your behaviour. They are deep-rooted in your being and reflect what is important and meaningful in your life. Your values are there to guide your decisions, actions and ultimately, your life's direction. If you have lost a sense of your values, if these are not being upheld in your life, then undoubtedly you will experience feelings of low self-worth and self-esteem.

To clarify, self-worth is about knowing and believing your worth as a person, knowing you have something to offer, whilst self-esteem is how you think and feel about yourself. If you don't appreciate or know what you have to offer, it is difficult to acknowledge your worth. If you don't have a clear sight of your values, you are unlikely to feel a sense of empowerment and control, leading to feelings of not being good enough.

Positive psychology studies have found that individuals who actively identify and live in alignment with their values tend to have an increased sense of life satisfaction, enhanced well-being, and greater resilience. When your daily activity is congruent with your values, you experience a profound sense of authenticity and contentment, which evokes feelings of belonging and worth, a feeling of purpose in your presence.

Defining your values is a deeply reflective and introspective process which you may find challenging. Values are the essence of who you are, so take time to explore what truly matters to you. Let them guide you on your journey, enabling you to live a more enriching and meaningful life. Here are some questions and considerations you may wish to reflect on when identifying your core values:

Take time for self-reflection and consider the qualities and principles that you hold in high regard. What are the beliefs that guide your life? Consider what makes you feel a sense of pride and ask yourself why. Explore moments when you feel compromised, moments when you may feel sad or angry. This reflection and awareness will help to pinpoint your values. If you struggle to get to the core of your values, invite others to share with you what values they see you upholding. What do you think they would say? Is that in alignment with your beliefs about yourself?

Sometimes, gaining clarity on your values can prove difficult and you may be uncertain in knowing whether these are your values or have been placed there by others and the experiences you have encountered. Social and cultural expectations can shape our values, leading us to become disconnected between our true values and our sense of what we *"should"* value. Challenge these influences by asking yourself why this value is important to you. Connect with how that value makes you feel when it is upheld and how it feels when this value is breached.

You may find your inner critic challenging values that appear contradictory, for example, many feel conflicted by values around their career and family aspirations. Rather than forgoing your values, challenge the self-limiting belief that tells you these cannot co-exist. If you are finding values clash, explore in more detail what the value means to you and how it would show up in your life. In a world where anything is possible, how would those values co-exist? Remember, you are not inviting others to pass judgement on you or your values, this is all about you, and other people's opinions are, after all, none of your business.

In defining your values, you may come to the realisation that certain aspects of your life don't align. This can cause fear and uncertainty. Now's not the time to run and give up; now is the time to self-soothe, acknowledge the fear, show yourself some compassion and use the tools you packed in your Happya Survival Kit. Defining your values requires vulnerability and honesty with yourself, which can be uncomfortable. It is natural to encounter challenges along the way. Be patient with yourself and allow your values to evolve as you continue to learn and grow.

Once you understand the values that underpin who you are, it's time to explore what ignites your passion. Uncovering your passion starts with self-reflection. Consider the activities and pursuits that fill you with joy and enthusiasm. Explore what activities make you feel most alive and fulfilled. When you engage in your passions you will find yourself in a state of flow, where your mind is completely immersed in an activity - that time when you can let go of everything you have on your to-do list, and you can just be in the moment. Your passions are unique to you, shaped by your experiences, and interests. They may include creative pursuits like writing, art and music, or more professional pursuits, sports, or general hobbies. Some of these would have been identified when you packed your Happya Survival Kit. Remember, finding your passion is a deeply personal journal. It's about being open to exploration, embracing your unique self and staying aligned with your values.

Embrace your curiosity and explore new interests. Sometimes your passions won't be discovered if you become trapped with overthinking. Trying new activities, taking up hobbies or delving into subjects of interest may offer the spark of interest that you are looking for. You may also find it beneficial to consider what you most enjoyed in childhood before life and responsibility seemingly took up so much time. Be patient with yourself, your passions can evolve, and you change as you grow. Sometimes, we can hold onto beliefs that stop us from following a passion. Perhaps you loved painting but were told you weren't good enough, that's no reason to stop! You can still paint; it is not for anyone else, it's your passion. This isn't a task that will be completed in an hour. It is something to reflect upon over the course of your journey, a topic for you to consider involved in daily life. Take notice of activities that provide positive emotions. Take notice of others. Are they engaging in activities that hold interest to you? If it's something you'd want to do but you can't see how you could achieve it, don't dismiss it, make a note of it, put it on your vision board and when the time is right you will find a way. Saying yes to your dreams is covered in Chapter Eight.

Understanding your passions provides further insight into your values. Engaging in your passions should be in harmony with living your values. For example, if you value self-expression and creativity, your passion may be painting. Dedicate time to journaling about the activities that bring you the most joy and fulfilment. Engage in conversations with friends and family about their observations of when you appear to be at your most happy. Really get a sense of what it is about the activity, sometimes we get caught up in the task itself when really you need to connect with the emotion and the somatic sensations in your body.

Now it's time to bring these two aspects together to build clarity about what holds meaning and purpose. By exploring what you have learned, consider where there is alignment between your values and your passions. Consider all the activities in your life and consider whether these are in alignment with your values and passions. Reflect on how much time and energy you are giving to activities that are out of alignment and consider how you can adapt these or perhaps stop them. Perhaps there are activities you started out of a sense of obligation which, now you are on this transformative journey, it is time to let go of. Also, consider where there are gaps. Perhaps you find that some of your values and passions don't currently have an outlet. For example, if you value education but are not engaged in any learning activities, it would be beneficial to explore how such activities can be included in your pursuits.

Positive psychology shows that those who live purposefully tend to experience greater life satisfaction, improved mental health, and well-being. Having a greater understanding of your values and passions can steer your choices and inform your decisions, enabling you to live a more meaningful and purposeful life. To maintain your focus and keep you in alignment, a personal mission statement can be your north star in guiding your life's journey. This is a deeply personal statement and should be clear and concise and provide a source of inspiration. Start with a statement of what drives you and what you want to achieve in your life. Next, outline your core values and how they will serve you in your life's journey. Describe how you will expend your energy on your passions in alignment with your values. Finish your statement with an inspiring statement of why you are doing this. Why have you made the decision to live a happya life? What would it mean to you?

Remember, your statement is not fixed, you can adapt it as you grow, and it will be something to revisit as you continue your journey of self-discovery. The tasks in this book are not one-off exercises but activities you can repeat as you and your life evolve, and you gain a greater understanding of your own identity.

Now let's explore your self-belief. Your self-belief empowers you to embark on this transformative journey with confidence and feelings of empowerment. Just as your values and passions provide the direction, self-belief provides the confidence.

Self-belief, also referred to as self-efficacy, is the unwavering belief in your ability to shape your life positively. It's the assurance that you possess the competence, resilience and capacity to navigate your life's journey. It determines your ability to realise your dreams and aspirations. Self-belief is important because it serves as a catalyst for empowerment. If you believe in yourself and your ability to make choices that are in alignment with who you are - to do the things that you value and follow your passions - you will take more decisive and aligned action. You are not a passive observer in your life but are able to orchestrate your success and the trajectory of your life.

Positive psychology shows us that those with higher self-belief can maintain a more positive outlook on life. When faced with challenges and adversity they are viewed as opportunities for growth rather than barriers to fulfilment in their life. In essence, self-belief fuels you to live your life authentically. Without that fuel, you aren't going anywhere fast and will find yourself in a constant battle. But how do you cultivate self-belief? Here are some suggestions to get you started. Remember, it takes time, practice and consistency to embed change so be patient with yourself and you can be assured of the results.

Creating a list of positive affirmations will boost self-belief. These should be practised daily. Have visual reminders placed around your house, a post-it note on your mirror is a great reminder. Perhaps you can have your affirmation saved onto your phone lock screen, "I am enough", "I am capable", or "I am strong". It's important to select something that is meaningful and resonates with you.

Celebrate your achievements, no matter how small. This reinforces your belief in your abilities. By keeping a success journal and documenting your achievements, you will soon start to see this build and realise how much you handle in your life. It is easy to forget the small, less sensational bits from the list, but just like with trauma, it is not about the event itself but in this case, the energy it takes. For some, making a phone call or getting out of the house may take their entire day's energy, for others it may be getting a promotion. All things are worth noting.

To further embed and charge your self-belief, consider your personal strengths. Recognise your strengths and talents, your natural abilities and the qualities that make you the person you are. It is also just as important to recognise the areas you know aren't your natural strength because it's important that you love and accept your whole self. Whilst some of you will be expert timekeepers, others of you will have a reputation for always being late! Some will be organised whilst others chaotic. It is the combination of both that makes you uniquely you and owning all of you is empowering. You can easily recognise where you can make progress and find opportunities to leverage your strengths whilst also knowing the areas where you need to call in others or find resources to support you at different times. Nobody can be everything!

To help you assess your strengths, you can do some self-reflection and get some feedback from supportive friends and family to give you input you may overlook. Alternatively, you can undertake an online strengths assessment such as the VIA Survey of Character Strengths, see https://www.viacharac ter.org/ for further information. Your strengths are integral to your authentic self and leveraging them and acknowledging them alongside those areas where you aren't so adept enables you to feel in control of your own life improving your well-being, setting you up for success.

In assessing your strengths, it is important to align them with your personality. Your personality influences how you see and interact with the world around you. There are lots of different personality assessment tests available, such as the Big Five Personality test www.bigfive-test.com. Try out one of these tests or, alternatively, undertake some self-reflection. Consider your role models and the personality traits you admire in them. What aspects do you resonate with? Explore your personal preferences - are you an extrovert or an introvert? How do you recharge your energy, is it in isolation or amongst people? If you get stuck ask your closest allies what three core personality traits they would use to describe you.

In this chapter of self-discovery, we've sought to uncover the inner you, the one that has been hidden for some time. Now you have peeled back the layers and begun to recognise your values, passions and strengths, you can begin to foster the self-belief to achieve your happya life, a life where your authentic self is in alignment with the life you are leading. You've uncovered the pieces of who you are and as we continue this journey, you will begin to see a picture coming together of your vision for the future.

At the heart of this exploration are your values, the guiding principles that show you the way. Your values keep you on course, ensuring your actions are aligned with your authentic self. As you continue your journey, keep your values at the forefront of your mind and recognise how they are showing up daily. If you identify parts of your life that are out of alignment, consider how you can adjust so you don't go off course.

Your happya life awaits, and it begins with you. This chapter, whilst it takes a limited time to read, will take a lot more time to implement and for change to take place. It starts with taking the first step and having faith in the process. The tools and techniques are not isolated activities. They will continue to hold value and in revisiting them, you will take something new each time. Each time you uplevel your life, take on a new challenge or simply over the course of time, you may wish to check in to ensure you aren't holding onto beliefs that aren't yours.

"Your emotions make you human. Even the unpleasant ones have a purpose. Don't lock them away. If you ignore them, they just get louder and angrier."

— SABBA TAHIR

Chapter 5

Acknowledge Your Emotions

Armed with a greater understanding of who you are, it's time to equip yourself with the skills you need to navigate your journey. Having been through so much and having survived for so long, taking control of your emotions can seem like an impossible feat. In this chapter, we will explore your emotional landscape - how your emotions are influencing your thoughts, behaviours, actions and relationships. Learning how to understand and embrace your emotions and improve your emotional intelligence, will support you in navigating life's challenges on your journey to fulfilment. It is only when you can fully acknowledge your emotions and manage them effectively that you can live an authentic life and find your happya.

If you have struggled to acknowledge and process your emotions, it can often feel as though your emotions are in control of you. Even when your conscious thought is suggesting you should be happy, your emotions may be offering up a different story. This can be extremely frustrating and confusing.

When emotions become confusing and overwhelming, people will often attempt to bury or distract themselves in the hope that, over time, they will fade. However, as is often said, if you bury something alive, it is going to come back and inevitably, your emotions will find another way of making you listen. The issue, however, is that by the time you have got to this point, not only will your emotions be supercharged, but they will also have become detached from the original initiating event or circumstance, meaning the message they hold can become confused. The more emotions are ignored, the more complex they will become and the more difficult it will be to understand their origin to the point that the event at which the emotion first occurred may no longer be in your conscious memory bank.

For those who have unprocessed trauma, emotions can appear to be your adversary, taking over your life and showing up in unexpected ways. Trauma can also magnify your emotions, making life feel like a roller coaster of highs and lows, becoming more extreme and difficult to handle. However, your emotions are your allies, akin to your inner critic discussed in Chapter Three. In this chapter, you will be guided to understand and acknowledge your emotions so you can process and learn from them.

So, what are your emotions and why do we have them? Your emotions are a blend of thoughts, sensations and responses to your perceptions and experiences of the world around you. They form the bridge between your inner self and the outer world. Your emotions offer insight into your inner world. They are the messages of your true self that your conscious self may overlook. Your emotions are there to tell you the underlying story of the beliefs you are holding. They play an essential role in communicating your needs and support you in aligning your actions with your passions and values.

Emotions themselves are not easily described as our interpretation of them becomes complex in its detail and your views are subjective, based on your identity and your experiences. However, more easily recognisable are the core emotions, anger, disgust, fear, joy, sadness, and surprise. Anger is a strong and intense emotion and usually manifests itself along with threat or injustice. When experiencing anger, it can manifest itself with a physiological response of an increased heart rate and tension. As your mind interprets the core feeling of anger, it may provide further descriptors such as frustration or hostility. Disgust is a reaction to offensive and unpleasant stimulation; it can manifest as rejection and can be further interpreted as disdain or contempt, for example. Fear is a response to danger or uncertainty and can trigger the fight or flight response, causing a physiological reaction. As the mind processes fear it may present as anxiety, panic or nervousness. Joy is associated with happiness and pleasure and is manifested in smiling and laughter. In the cognitive processing of joy, it may be described as bliss or elation. Sadness is a response to loss, disappointment and unmet expectations. It can manifest itself through tears and frowning. As it's processed, it may be explained as grief, regret or despair. Surprise is a reaction to unexpected events; your physical reaction may be jaw-dropping and a widening of your eyes. On reflection, it may be described as astonishment or disbelief.

There are many ways in which the core emotions can be interpreted. There are also times when different core emotions will merge, making them more complex. For example, imagine someone who is committed to their job, works hard and invests time and effort into everything they do but perceives a lack of recognition or reward. The individual may experience anger from the injustice and in response to the perceived wrongdoing. Simultaneously, they may also experience sadness from a sense of disappointment or feelings of not being enough. This combination of anger and sadness may present as resentment.

Overall, your emotions are a part of your life experience and act as an internal messaging system throughout your body. Whilst often misinterpreted, they have a vital role to play in keeping you safe, maintaining your well-being and bringing you joy. They have the power to elevate you as well as plunge you into uncertainty. Essentially, they also signal whether your actions are in alignment with your authentic self and your happya life. If emotions are good for you, if they are simply there to protect and deliver the messages of how our needs and wants are or are not being met, why do they cause such an issue?

Problems occur when your emotions are left unheard or if you experience emotional overwhelm. If your emotions have been signalling to you that there is an issue and you continue to ignore them, they just get more complex and try harder to be heard. Perhaps your emotions have been ignored because other things or people have been given priority, perhaps your needs have not been met in some way. If you have neglected your self-care, you will feel a range of emotions to signal these needs require tending to. If you carry on ignoring them, not only are you starving yourself of that energy, but you are also ignoring your messaging system. When you ignore the message, your mind and body believe the signalling is not working, so the emotion grows stronger in order to be heard. Ultimately, ignoring your emotions lowers your self-worth and is detrimental to your well-being. Often, we can be encouraged to ignore our emotions. Some of you may have been in situations where you were told your feelings and emotions weren't important or they risked your safety. Reflect now on the times you have been told your emotions aren't valid.

Societal norms, well-intentioned caregivers and those who form part of our community can convey messages that undermine the validity of emotions. Were you told, *"It's wicked to want"*, *"There's nothing to be scared of monsters aren't real"*, *"You're over-reacting, they're just kids"*, *"Life's not fair, get used to it"*, *"It's not the end of the world, don't be so dramatic"*, *"Calm down, you're being too loud"*? It's not just in childhood that we hear these messages. They continue into adulthood, *"Cheer up, it's not that bad"*, *"you're making other people sad"*, *"You're overreacting"*. Perhaps you now don't speak up about injustices or when things are wrong through fear of consequences. Ignoring your emotions can become confusing.

Your emotional well-being can also be significantly impacted by trauma. The intensity of the emotions experienced can be overwhelming, and the brain can shut down to protect itself from overload. The amygdala, the region of the brain responsible for emotional processing can become hypersensitive. This increased level of sensitivity can lead to exaggerated responses. The prefrontal cortex, responsible for emotional regulation can also become impaired, resulting in an individual becoming stuck in a perpetual cycle of fear. It isn't as simple as knowing that a danger has passed, you have to allow your body and cognitive functioning to catch up too. Being stuck in a perpetual state of alert is simply exhausting. Whilst some treatments can help with the symptoms, if the underlying issue is not resolved the symptoms will simply find a different outlet to make themselves heard.

Many people believe their inability to recover is down to some form of weakness in their personality, but the reality is their brain may have made that recovery impossible until the central nervous system has been calmed. Individuals who have experienced trauma will have a heightened sense of fear and anxiety. They may experience sadness and grief, anger, shame, guilt, numbness and detachment, along with so much more. It is no wonder that people will often try and avoid their own emotions.

Given all these factors, trying to get to grips with your emotions can feel excessive. Your emotions become so intertwined it is difficult to know where to start. You may become fearful of experiencing feelings of joy as you anticipate it will soon be followed by a surge of negative emotions flooding your body. You may try and hide your emotions deep inside in the hope that, over time, they will dissipate, and you will be okay. Perhaps you're just tired and want to leave them until you are stronger. Maybe you believe that by giving them attention, you will somehow empower them, and they will take even more control over your well-being.

If your emotions are left unchecked, they will become unwieldy, and their messages will be entangled and confused. This does not mean you are broken, nor does it mean you are a problem, or you are defunct. It simply means you need to do some decluttering of all the unwanted emotions because some of them won't be yours to hold onto and you need to do some general maintenance and upkeep. This is where your survival kit is crucial in working through your emotions so you can get to manage them much more efficiently and effectively.

One important myth to cover here is the validity of your emotions. All your emotions are valid and relevant, and your emotions are your own. Your experience and intensity of an emotion depends on your mind, body and soul's perception of a situation or experience. It is as individual as you are so you cannot expect everyone to respond and react in the same way. There is no right or wrong. Remember the discussion about "normal"? It is simply a consensus, and it does not determine right from wrong. You get to own your emotions and nobody else can tell you any different because they do not have that insight to give.

There are also no right or wrong emotions. Anger, jealousy and sadness are not wrong. Happiness, love and amusement are not right. Positive emotions are those that bring you pleasure whilst negative emotions generally bring discomfort. Positive psychology acknowledges all emotions and has scientifically proven the importance of negative emotions in an individual's growth journey. It is often, our negative emotions that provide the more valuable lessons - they have something to say. Perhaps it can be a warning of danger, of deviating from the plan or boundaries being challenged but also, they highlight the areas where you have a need requiring some attention and without that attention being given, you are likely to struggle with being successful.

Anger is often an emotion that comes up as being uncomfortable. Often people can feel guilty for being angry, as though it means they aren't a nice person if they feel anger. However, anger is only a problem when it transforms from an emotion to a behaviour. It is perfectly relevant to feel anger when someone or something violates your personal boundaries. It is only when we don't uphold our boundaries or listen to our emotions that anger can become exaggerated and result in unwanted behaviours.

Your emotions serve a purpose, are valid and perform an essential role in your well-being. Being able to recognise, acknowledge and understand the messages they are bringing enables you to respond to life in a more conscious and deliberate way. Your ability to perceive, understand and manage your emotions is pivotal for your well-being and success in life. Being able to process your emotions reaps other rewards too, as not only will your relationship with yourself be improved but it will also strengthen other relationships, enabling you to communicate more effectively and show empathy and compassion for others, creating a space for open dialogue and connection. This is referred to as your emotional intelligence. It starts with recognising and understanding your emotions, including their cause and the impact they are having. Next is to manage and control your emotions in different situations, such as staying calm under pressure, handling stress and responding to challenges in a way that upholds your values and achieves your desired results. Your emotions also serve to provide motivation towards achieving your goals, empathy for others, helping you understand other perspectives, and helping to effectively build positive relationships.

Whilst listening to your emotions is essential it is essential to note they are not meant to make decisions for you. Emotions provide valuable information about your internal needs and wants but they are not always in alignment with your rational state of mind. Your decisions should be made on a balance of emotional intelligence and cognitive rationale. Rather than making decisions based solely on an emotional reaction, that decision should also be subjected to reflective thought and assessment. You may be able to resonate here in identifying different approaches to decision-making in those around you. Think about that impulse purchase when shopping – sometimes, unfortunately, we can't just buy the thing we love, we have to give some consideration to its practical application (although not always! Sometimes a treat is good for the soul!).

Now that you hold a greater understanding of emotions, what are the strategies you can employ for processing and releasing emotions? Here are some effective strategies to help you in the management of emotions that are also effective in the healing of emotional trauma.

Firstly, and perhaps most often explored, is journaling. Writing down your emotions can help you gain clarity and perspective over your emotions. It enables you to identify the cause and impact and apply cognitive processing. The writing process itself can be cathartic, however, it may not offer the support other strategies can offer as it is done in isolation. It can, in some cases, encourage overthinking and cause a spiralling effect of emotions - causing emotions to become disproportionate. If this is the case, then it would be wise to seek an alternative approach. That said, journal prompts can be a useful starting point (and there are some included in the bonus resources), so it is beneficial to explore as you process. Set aside some time to write freely about your experiences, emotions and observations. This is your private space for self-reflection.

Alternatively, engaging in mindfulness and meditation practices can bring awareness to the present moment. This can particularly support the reduction of stress and help with emotional regulation. It may be difficult to practice in the first instance if you are experiencing emotional overwhelm. Observing your emotions and how they are impacting you will assist you in accepting and recognising the impact life is having upon you. Focus on your breath, note the sensations in your body and just allow yourself time and space when nothing else is demanding your attention.

Another common technique is practising gratitude. By focusing on positive aspects of your life, you can shift the focus from what is lacking to what is present and valuable in your life, helping you process and let go of what is no longer serving you or relevant in this chapter of your life. This does require consistent practice but is not something that should prove difficult to integrate into daily life.

Using positive affirmations can counteract negative self-talk and reinforce a positive mindset. If not believed though, they can lack real impact and may not address deeper issues. If the affirmations are not working for you, it may be beneficial to explore why and what is coming up when processing the affirmation through other techniques.

Another very effective approach is cognitive restructuring or reframing. This is a therapeutic approach that involves challenging negative thought patterns, beliefs and attitudes, causing an emotional response. By identifying the negative patterns and understanding your inner rationale you will become able to reframe and replace with a more balanced perspective, encouraging positive thoughts and behaviours.

Other practices for you to explore include creative expression, physical exertion, breathwork, muscle relaxation, emotional freedom technique or tapping, and hypnotherapy. All these techniques have been scientifically proven to support individuals in the processing and management of emotions. There is no right or wrong, it is about what works for you. It will take time to adjust to some of these techniques, so approach them with an open mind and allow yourself to fully embrace the experience.

Given a clearer understanding of emotions, their role in your well-being and the strategies for managing and processing your emotions, it's time for you to reflect and gain an understanding of where your emotions are controlling you and what improvements you can make. First, it is important to change your mindset about your emotions being a problem you'd rather deal with on another day. Empower yourself with the belief that you can take control. Gain an awareness of your emotions and the shifts in your mood. Identify circumstances where specific emotions arise. Practice mindfulness to help stay grounded in the moment and observe your thoughts around your emotions without judgement. At this stage, it is important to get clear on the message they must deliver and the belief from which they stem. Identify the triggers for your emotions. What environments, people or demands placed upon you trigger emotional responses? Understanding this will help you to take the appropriate action to anticipate, manage and release emotions in a healthy way. Learn from your emotions about what needs, values or boundaries are being impacted. As you start to take control of your emotional well-being and your emotional intelligence begins to increase, you will start to notice an increase in your self-worth.

In essence, your emotions are not your adversaries, they are not something to be fearful of and you do not need to run and hide from them or banish them from your thought process. They are there to help you stay on the path to achieving your goals, to ensure your needs are met and you remain authentic to yourself, your values, beliefs and passions. They carry wisdom and guidance and an ability to steer you away from danger. By proactively managing your emotions, you unlock their value, highlighting where you risk going off course, providing the motivation to take necessary actions and fuelling you to take the next step. Even when your emotions seem to conflict with your goals, they hold the answer to the limiting belief that may jeopardise your success. It is time to embrace your emotional well-being and take control. If your emotions are running wild, show them compassion and understanding and provide the necessary reassurance to calm and gain an understanding of the triggers. Remember, all emotions hold value and opportunity. Having control over your emotions significantly enhances your well-being and your potential for success. It enhances your relationships, optimises your decision-making, increases productivity, improves your physical well-being, enables resilience in times of adversity, is a key component of personal growth, enables effective communication, supports you with conflict resolution and encourages a positive influence on others. Having control over your emotions empowers you to navigate through life with purpose.

In the next chapter, we will be exploring boundaries, as we further expand on your ability to protect and show up as your authentic self. Whilst the work undertaken around emotions helps to understand and ensure your needs and values are being met, your boundaries serve to protect your emotional well-being to allow you to flourish.

"Love yourself enough to set boundaries: Your time and energy are precious.

You get to choose how you use it.

You teach people how to treat you by deciding what you will and won't accept."

— ANNA TAYLOR

CHAPTER 6

PRESERVE YOUR SPACE

I n this next chapter, we will uncover the importance of healthy boundaries, explore what they look like and how you can start to implement and uphold some healthier boundaries in your life. Let's start with how it feels if you haven't got healthy boundaries in place. If you find yourself doing things because you "*should*" as it's the polite thing to do, or because you feel obligated, there's room for improvement. If you are worried about other's judgement if you say no or don't volunteer your support, you could be struggling to uphold them. If you're making decisions based on everyone else's needs and ignoring your own, there are some boundaries that need to be acknowledged. If trying to communicate your needs and wants to others is leaving you feeling overwhelmed, resentful, exhausted and exploited, it's time to work on developing some healthy boundaries. It's time to say yes to what you want and no to everything else! It's time to make a paradigm shift to reclaim your space in a way that feels empowering, authentic and liberating.

Whilst the thought of saying no and standing your ground may feel overwhelming, that's okay, it's a skill you probably haven't utilised for a long time. It's not just your physical muscles that need nurture and exercise to maintain their strength, but your mental well-being needs exercising too. Remember Chapter Two, your energy can't be left stagnant, however, you can be assured that once you start exercising your boundary muscles it will all start to come together. Remember how we said there would be times when things would feel uncomfortable? These feelings aren't signalling it's time to run but your signal that something new is going to happen and, after all, new and different is what you signed up for! If you are feeling those jelly wobbles, check back in with the commitment you made to yourself in Chapter One and remember, this book and the bonus resources available to you are here to support and guide you to finding the balance that is right for you. Don't forget to reach into your Happya Survival Kit if you find your well-being challenged.

The importance of boundaries cannot be understated; however, it is about balance. You need to feel safe, but you also have a need to be you and to allow yourself space to bloom. Boundaries are essential for your self-care; without them, you leave little room to tend to your own needs, which can lead to overwhelm, burnout and stress. Boundaries also provide space for your unique identity to be represented in the world. If your true self isn't allowed to take up space, it will fundamentally undermine your self-worth and self-esteem. Your boundaries also protect your self-respect and communicating to others what you consider to be acceptable behaviour encourages them to treat you with respect too. They are the foundation of healthy relationships, provide context to prevent conflict, reduce stress, provide clarity and, importantly, prevent exploitation, enable personal growth, and empower you to make choices aligned with your values, beliefs, emotions and goals. Have I convinced you of their importance?

However, boundaries are not merely a set of rules to follow, neither are they meant to be high, thick walls built around you to keep you hidden and protected from a dangerous world. They are not meant to be built so strong that nothing can infiltrate them. Those are not healthy boundaries. Healthy boundaries enable you to be seen, and for you to see and interpret the world as you experience it. Your boundaries are there to filter, not block. Upholding your boundaries is about saying yes to the things you want and no to the things you don't want. However, life isn't as simple as right or wrong, despite your nervous system trying to categorise everything in the world as good or bad, safe or unsafe. The things that take courage, help you grow; you may need to step out of your comfort zone and, on occasion, through conscious choice, push beyond some of your boundaries. It is by doing things differently that you make progress and by being open to new opportunities, you can realise your potential to uplevel. If your boundaries are rigid, then it will result in you becoming closed off and you risk missing out on developing a richness to your life. It's all about maintaining the optimal balance and aligning your boundaries with your authentic self, whilst also challenging yourself to grow and take the next step.

Let's start by visualising your boundaries as a bubble around you. Imagine a transparent bubble, letting in the things you want in your life whilst everything else remains on the outside. Your bubble protects you and your energy whilst ensuring you remain connected to the outside world therefore maintaining your wellbeing. The bubble provides you with space for reflection and personal growth and allows you to re-energise and take time for yourself. It is only when you choose to allow something through that it can come into your world.

If you are recovering from the consequences of trauma. If you are experiencing feelings of insecurity and still finding your sense of stability, then you may want and need to envisage a bubble that is stronger and bigger, providing you with more space while you recover. Imagine you've got sunburn. Whilst your skin recovers you need to cover up and use some after sun. Whilst you're healing, you need to avoid anything that irritates or hinders your recovery, instead opting for the soothing tools from within your survival kit. However, for those of you whose skin has recovered but are still covering up and hiding from the rest of the world, it is time to start allowing the world to come a little closer. It is time to remove walls and barricades so you can be seen, but this needs to be done with self-compassion so as not to trigger your nervous system. It's about taking it one step at a time in steps that feel okay or perhaps even slightly uncomfortable. If you have your survival kit alongside you, it will enable you to navigate your journey in the right direction.

As you become more confident in yourself and in upholding your boundaries you will find yourself more competent at negotiation and refining your boundaries to allow new opportunities to filter through. If you are testing some boundaries and stepping out of your comfort zone, consider how you can support yourself by utilising the tools and techniques in your survival kit. Perhaps you have someone in your life who you find quite challenging or find it particularly difficult to say no to; if that is the case, then it may be beneficial to uphold a tighter boundary with them whilst giving yourself the strength to build. Remember, set yourself up for success by facing potential challenges prepared.

Whilst boundaries are there to protect you, they are also essential for maintaining a healthy connection with the world and positive relationships with people in your community. Without them, it is easy to become consumed by the demands of others, leading to burnout and overwhelm. By understanding your boundaries, you can preserve your personal identity and empower yourself to communicate your needs, assert your values and navigate your life with integrity and transparency. By setting healthy boundaries, you can prioritise your own well-being, maintaining the fine balance between giving and taking. They are also there to protect you and your energy, enabling you to feel safe and to expend your energy on pursuits that are aligned with your values and dreams. Setting them is an act of self-love and encourages self-worth, empowering you to be confident in your actions and in achieving a greater sense of control in your life.

There are several different types of boundaries for you to consider, each addressing different aspects of your life. They include physical, intellectual, emotional, sexual, material and time boundaries. For each of these categories, take some time to contemplate what your boundaries are, how well you uphold them and where you believe changes may need to be made.

Physical boundaries incorporate your personal space and physical touch. They're about feeling comfortable with how close others get to be with you whilst ensuring your comfort. Protecting your physical boundaries is essential for your personal safety, comfort and sense of autonomy. Upholding these boundaries can be challenging where there are differing cultural norms, social pressure or even fear of conflict. However, if you don't uphold your boundaries on your terms, you can be left feeling violated, uncomfortable or unsafe in your own space or body. If you feel physically threatened by someone, find support and take action to protect yourself. Be clear on your physical boundaries and take action to protect yourself.

Intellectual boundaries, are about being respectful of your thoughts and ideas, allowing you to maintain your authentic perspective. Upholding them promotes open communication and allows your opinions to be heard. If they are not upheld, it can lead to difficult relationships and a lack of trust. Suppressing your thoughts and ideas can create a perceived disconnect between your words and actions. Examples of intellectual boundaries not being upheld include avoiding debates and being under pressure to conform to others' opinions. Upholding your intellectual boundaries will help boost your self-esteem as your thoughts and ideas get validation and acceptance.

Emotional boundaries consider your feelings and protect your emotional well-being and how much you share with others. Upholding your emotional boundaries supports you in emotional regulation, ensures your emotional well-being and enables healthy relationships. Examples include communicating your feelings honestly and respectfully, acknowledging how you feel, allowing yourself the space to process them, validating your sense of self and acknowledging the impact experiences and interactions have on you. Often, we fail to uphold these boundaries through fear of rejection, guilt, and focusing on other's needs and opinions over our own.

Sexual boundaries represent your desires and limitations. Sexual boundaries determine what level of intimacy you are and aren't comfortable with. Clearly communicating your boundaries will help to protect you from feeling violated. Again, this is a particular area where you may wish to enlist support from others or specialist resources.

Material boundaries account for your possessions and money, considering what, when and how you share. Examples include setting a budget and sticking to it, and being clear about your expectations when sharing your material belongings. Not upholding these boundaries can lead to financial stress, conflict and feelings of being taken advantage of. These boundaries are often compromised by feelings of guilt, fear of appearing selfish and pressure from others.

Finally, time boundaries preserve how you share and employ your time. They prevent burnout and ensure you allocate your time according to your priorities. Examples include finding the time for self-care and saying no to taking on other responsibilities when your schedule is already full. The consequences of not upholding your time boundaries are feelings of overwhelm and exhaustion, and self-neglect. It is often fear of disappointing others, engaging in people-pleasing or an excessively busy lifestyle that challenges these boundaries.

In summary, each type of boundary is essential to maintain your physical and mental well-being. They preserve your unique self and help foster connection and healthy relationships with others. They may feel uncomfortable whilst you get used to putting them in place and enforcing them when challenged, but they are protecting you from the negative consequences of stress, overwhelm and low self-esteem, to name just a few.

When considering each of these areas, ensure your boundaries are built on the foundations of your identity so that you uphold your values and beliefs whilst remaining authentic to yourself. In setting your boundaries, you must strive to achieve a balance between asserting your needs and the feelings of others. Showing compassion for yourself and for others enables you to build respectful relationships.

Setting your boundaries may feel challenging however the work you have undertaken in previous chapters should provide some clarity on where to focus your attention. Cultivating self-awareness provides the foundation for setting boundaries that resonate with your authentic self. Begin by taking some time for self-reflection. Consider the work you have completed and what you have already learned. Reflect on how your values and beliefs can be upheld by each of the different types of boundaries: physical, intellectual, emotional, sexual, material and time. For example, if honesty is a core value, consider an intellectual boundary around open and honest communications with those around you.

Consider situations that make you feel uncomfortable and identify what needs to be in place to enable you to feel safe and ensure your needs are met. Perhaps you can recall times when your boundaries were breached - how did this make you feel? what could you have done differently? Consider both past experiences and your current circumstances - where do you feel your boundaries have been crossed or where they have not been upheld?

Be honest about your limits. Think about scenarios in which you feel uncomfortable, times when your boundaries have been stretched. Be aware of the impact this has had on you in the past and take note of how your discomfort is displayed. How does your nervous system respond? Do you go into fight, flight, freeze or fawn mode? How do you know you are feeling uncomfortable? Is it a feeling in your stomach or throat, do you start to perspire or stumble over your words? There is no right or wrong, just how it feels for you. Being aware of these signals will prepare you in the future and serve as a reminder to uphold your boundaries. You will need to reflect on these areas in consideration of all the different relationships you hold as well as other factors such as the environment you are in. For example, some find public displays of affection make them feel uncomfortable whilst for others it feels completely natural.

Once you have started to determine your boundaries it's time to communicate them to those around you. Communicating them clearly, assertively, and without apology is key to establishing trust and respect which in turn leads to stronger and closer relationships. To avoid conflict, use "I" statements, ensuring your message is positioned as your perspective and expectation reducing the potential of a defensive response or leaving room for challenge. For example, *"I need some time alone to recharge"* is more effective than saying *"You are always in my space"*.

Always ensure you are respectful of others when communicating your boundaries and be careful to avoid blame. Crucially, consistency is key. If you aren't committed to upholding your boundaries, others around you won't see them as important. It is also necessary to remain open to others' views as sometimes, their views may offer a different perspective and provide an opportunity to adapt, which is very different to giving in or succumbing to others' demands.

It is equally important and powerful in boundary setting to learn to say "no". Getting comfortable with declining invitations or requests that don't align with your boundaries is essential to managing your well-being and feelings of self-worth. It is important to not only find the confidence in saying no but also to do this respectfully and confidently to avoid conflict. Saying "no" helps preserve your time and energy. And remember, "no" is a whole sentence, there is no requirement placed on you to justify your decision-making.

As you become more aware of where you have previously been unable to communicate or uphold your boundaries, you may find it beneficial to determine some phrases to support you in situations where your boundaries may be challenged, some examples have been provided in the bonus materials for this chapter. For example, to protect an intellectual boundary you may use the phrase *"I appreciate your perspective, but I disagree"*. Communicating your boundaries clearly and respectfully establishes trust and respect which inevitably leads to stronger and closer relationships.

Upholding your boundaries often feels difficult and you can face some barriers when implementing and enforcing them, both from yourself and others. Fear of rejection is a significant barrier to change; it may feel safer to accept the status quo or consensus rather than upholding your boundary through fear of rejection or exclusion. Guilt and a sense of obligation to others' needs can hold you back. Perhaps a lack of self-esteem holds you back from recognising that your needs are as important as those of others.

Or maybe you lack assertiveness or struggle with communicating your emotions, perhaps you experience feelings of co-dependency. However, with determination, focus and the right mindset, these are all barriers that can be overcome.

Remember, you are going to have to be a little uncomfortable if you want change to happen and that means others are going to have to adjust too. But their adjustment and response are absolutely their responsibility - whilst you can influence how the message lands, their feelings and actions are theirs and theirs alone.

For some of you, it may be a case of testing the implementation of your boundaries in a safer way so begin with those who are closer to you and are more trusted, setting smaller goals or practising your assertiveness and saying no where there is lower risk. Call in trusted allies to support you and hold you accountable for upholding your boundaries. Setting boundaries is a learning process, be patient with yourself and remember, growth takes time. Treat yourself with the same compassion you treat others.

You may also find that whilst you are going through this transformative journey you find yourself feeling particularly challenged and your boundaries need to be placed further away to give yourself more space to heal. For example, if you have a friend who challenges you to take action that makes you feel uncomfortable and whilst you value their friendship, right now you don't have the energy to deal with their unsolicited opinions, you may want to uphold a stricter boundary that holds them further back from you whilst you get to grips with your own identity and thought process, giving you time to determine what you want. Once healed, and feeling more confident in handling conversations and situations, you can allow those people to gain more access to you and your life. Think about how some people will be kept close and are a part of your inner circle whilst others you have a more detached or distant relationship.

One of the most essential elements to support you in upholding your boundaries is through establishing and fostering a strong and supportive network. The people you surround yourself with play a pivotal role in your well-being and help preserve your sense of self. A supportive network provides validation; when you have people around you who respect your limits, it reinforces your self-belief and gives you confidence in upholding them with others. They provide you with emotional support and encouragement, a space to express your feelings and problem-solve. They hold you accountable for upholding your boundaries, and with an awareness of your goals and limits, they can provide a gentle reminder when allowing them to slip. They can also help support you when boundaries are breached by others. Your network can also provide role models, introducing you to different approaches for upholding boundaries. Choose your inner circle wisely and surround yourself with people who share your values and who respect your needs.

Not everyone in your current network may embrace the changes you are making. They may not identify with your need for something new or different, they may themselves be finding life challenging. Be patient but clear on your priorities. Whilst you may experience guilt for asserting your boundaries, remember that your well-being is your priority, and the right people will be right there alongside you. It may take time to find the right people but in the long term, you will be glad you did. You are never alone on this journey, there will always be others to support you, including in the happya community.

In this chapter, we've explored the significance of boundaries and how you can begin to implement and uphold healthier boundaries in your life. Whenever you find yourself doing something out of a sense of obligation or finding your own desires and aspirations are not being met, reflect on where your boundaries are not being upheld. In striving to achieve a happya life, it's essential to say yes to what truly resonates with you and no to everything else. It's time for you to reclaim your space and show the world the amazing individual that you are.

It's understandable if these changes feel overwhelming, so ensure you give yourself the self-love and compassion you need and make use of your survival kit throughout the journey. If you need a reminder of why you are doing this, look back on the work, you did in Chapter One, where you made the commitment to yourself to live your happya life.

Remember, boundaries are not rigid rules, and they are not written in stone, however, flexing them should be a conscious decision. Healthy boundaries are those that provide you with the space you need to re-energise, enable personal growth, and uphold your own values and beliefs. Ensure you give yourself the space you need especially if you are in a period of recovery or whilst you are undertaking a significant transformation. The work you are doing in this book takes time and energy and trying to do too much can become overwhelming. There is no timeline for implementation that is something you get to determine for yourself.

Ensure you have considered all types of boundaries, practise the art of saying no and give yourself permission to reflect on times when you feel your boundaries are being challenged or have been breached. Ultimately, boundaries are your allies in protecting you, preserving your authenticity and supporting your well-being. They are the key to unlocking stronger and more meaningful relationships and empowering you to live the life you design. So, let's begin your journey in a transparent bubble, allowing the beautiful world we live in to shine through whilst keeping out the unnecessary drama.

"No one escapes pain, fear and suffering. Yet from pain can come wisdom, from fear can come courage, from suffering can come strength."

— ERIC GREITENS

CHAPTER 7

PROCESS AND RELEASE

As you gain an appreciation for the real you, for the incredible human being you are and all that you have to offer the world, and in honouring the promise you made to yourself, it is time to let go of all that is not serving you. It is time to let go of all the things that you no longer need to hold onto. The act of processing and releasing is a vital step on your journey towards a happya life. This chapter is here to support you in healing from past traumas, releasing those limiting beliefs, and cultivating forgiveness on a quest for post-traumatic growth and the realisation of the happya life. It is not, however, a replacement for professional support and is only recommended to be attempted when you are in a place of mental stability. If you are struggling with daily life, I urge you to reach out to the resources in this book for personal support and guidance.

For those of you who are ready to move forward, be prepared. Given the topic and nature of this chapter, it's important to ensure you have the time and energy it requires to explore some of the issues whilst supporting yourself with your survival kit. It is surprising how much energy can be consumed in stopping and taking a moment for yourself. Never is it more important to ensure you have time dedicated to you.

We'll be exploring the traumas that have shaped your life to understand the hidden scars so you can begin the process of acknowledging them and understanding them, before letting them go. We'll be identifying those beliefs you hold about yourself and the world around you and begin to challenge and reframe them, allowing you to release yourself from feelings of being stuck and overwhelmed. Then, through forgiveness for yourself and others, and embracing compassion, you can challenge the narrative of the inner critic and replace judgement with self-love.

In the process of healing and growth, we'll reflect on how far you've come and celebrate you because you are enough, just as you are, and you deserve happiness, fulfilment and contentment. In moments of self-reflection, we can stumble across the realisation that the blocks we envisage in our lives are often not external to ourselves. Some of the greatest challenges we face come from deep within us. It is no wonder, when setting out to uncover our authentic self, we can find ourselves dancing with self-sabotage. Our inner-self, rallying the troops to protest, with their placards telling you that you're not good enough, you're too old, you're not important, you're not rich enough, you don't deserve it. Well, this is the moment to say no more! No longer are you going to allow those messages to consume you, no longer are you going to allow those words to stop you in your tracks. You've got this and you've made the commitment to go all in so let's get started.

In Chapter Three, you were introduced to the concept of the backpack you carry where you collect all your life's experiences, and you took some time to reflect on both positive and negative experiences that you carry with you on this journey. Now, we are going to further explore the adversity that you have experienced. Even long after a traumatic experience or painful memory from your past, you can continue to carry its burden. You become so accustomed to the weight that it becomes just part of your daily existence causing an unnecessary drain on your energy and resources. Perhaps you have scars left by a difficult childhood, a toxic relationship, personal loss or societal pressures and expectations. Acknowledging past traumas can be one of the most challenging, yet transformative steps in your journey towards a happya life.

Acknowledgement of these experiences is not about dwelling in the past, nor is it about attributing blame. It is about understanding how they have shaped your unconscious beliefs, behaviours and emotions. It's about bringing a sense of awareness to these unwritten rules that underpin your sense of control and influence, as well as your decision-making and the scope of choices you believe are available to you. To undertake this is going to require you to show courage and if you are already feeling depleted and overwhelmed, that might seem like a challenging task. How do you find the energy and courage to do something else when your energy levels are already low? It starts with managing your self-care, ensuring you have your survival kit alongside you for the journey. Offering yourself not only the compassion you deserve but also offering it to the younger version of yourself who endured those experiences. Giving the acknowledgement that they were doing the best they could at the time with the resources and knowledge they had. In particular, consider how experiences in your childhood were not your fault and how you weren't responsible for solving them. Now, you are older and wiser, now, you have time and resources available to support you and you can release yourself from that burden that was never yours to carry.

To support you in your healing journey, take some time to write a letter to your younger self. If you have experienced traumatic events, then you may find it beneficial to write to different aged versions of yourself. Perhaps it is beneficial to consider events at a young age, maybe five years old, then into teens and adulthood. Your experiences and journey are unique, so think about what best suits your circumstances. In this letter, offer words of understanding and comfort. Consider what that younger version of yourself needed to hear and offer them that now. Let them know that you are here for them and that you will always take care of them. Let them know you are now an adult and have made a commitment to yourself to never allow your authentic self to be left behind again, and that you have the wisdom and resources to keep them safe. This activity will bring up a lot of emotions and it's important that you allow space for them to rise whilst offering yourself the reassurance you need to know you are safe and loved. Consider what resources you packed in your survival kit to support your emotional well-being and ensure you give this area extra attention. Remember, you are not alone on this journey, and this is not a space where you are going to dwell. Due to the nature of this task, it is recommended to plan it at a time when you are fully energised and have your survival kit and support infrastructure in place. Give yourself the time and space you need to process the emotions that will come up. If you find it overwhelming, take a break and come back to it at another time. Remember, you have control of your emotions so listen to their message and then decide what action needs to be taken.

In taking the courageous step to acknowledge your past trauma and how it has shaped your life, you are better able to take on a transformation. It is time to face your limiting beliefs, those ingrained assumptions about the world that you have carried for far too long. It is in your power to change these beliefs so that you can release yourself from a life of survival and find your happya.

Your beliefs shape your thoughts, emotions and actions. Often, others' beliefs can become intertwined with your own identity, hence the previous chapters exploring your values, strengths, passions and personality. Those chapters were aimed at understanding your true self underneath the layers of conditioned beliefs. As you process and release your trauma, they are the are chapters you may wish to revisit as you start to view the world and your role within it differently, but first, we need to identify those limiting beliefs.

What are the stories you tell yourself? Often, they will manifest in the form of self-criticism, self-doubt, or fear of failure. The more common examples are:

I'm not good enough - a belief that can cause constant feelings of inadequacy.

I don't deserve happiness - stemming from feeling unworthy.

I'm powerless to change - feeling a lack of control and influence over your life.

I must be perfect - often rooted in a fear of making mistakes or risk-taking.

Take some time to consider what those beliefs are before moving forward with challenging and reframing them.

Consider the past experiences and what they taught you, and explore the thoughts and emotions connected with these situations. Take time to reflect on the key messages you have told yourself about these events.

A powerful exercise to undertake here is a body scan, a mindfulness practice that invites you to become aware of the sensations in your body. This is a non-judgmental practice that enables you to explore the deep connection between the mind and the body. The body scan can be a transformative tool in aiding the processing and healing of trauma. It can help release tension and improve your overall well-being. To begin, find a quiet and comfortable space. You can sit or lie down. Make sure you won't be interrupted and turn off any devices - this is going to be your time and anything else can wait.

Begin by grounding yourself in the moment, close your eyes if it feels comfortable to do so, take a few deep breaths and allow your body and mind to settle. Nobody wants anything and nobody needs anything. Now bring your attention to your breath. Focus on it. Notice the expansion and contraction of your abdomen with each inhale and exhale. Take a few moments to simply observe. Begin to feel your body relax and let go. When you are ready, with the next inhale it is time to start turning your attention to different parts of your body. With each inhale imagine sending that breath into a specific part of your body, for example, start with taking the breath down to your toes. Notice how the breath feels. Systematically, take each breath into all areas of the body and observe, without trying to change anything, the feelings and sensations you experience. It is common for thoughts and judgements to arise during this process. Acknowledge their presence and continue to focus on your breathing. As you complete the scan of your entire body, notice any changes you have experienced and when you are ready, bring yourself back to the present moment. Allow yourself some time to gently reflect on your observations and the stories they are telling you. Explore the nature of these sensations. You can use this technique to help review and release trauma from within your body and explore limiting beliefs further by understanding where in the body it is held.

When you are ready and have started to identify your limiting beliefs, it's time for you to process them, realising they are not facts, they are interpretations of a past story - a past story that doesn't need to define your future.

It's beneficial to journal different instances when you recognise limiting beliefs arising. Thinking about the situations, emotions and thoughts associated with the beliefs will help you become aware of different triggers and patterns of behaviour, enabling you to challenge and reframe them. As you educate yourself on these thoughts and behaviours, you will eventually be able to get ahead of them before they arise until eventually, they are no longer part of your being.

When you come across a particularly challenging limiting belief, challenge it by exploring what supporting evidence there is to back up the belief. Also, note the evidence that contradicts the belief.

To help release the belief you can use affirmations to counter them. Repeat these affirmations regularly. Emotional Freedom Technique (EFT), otherwise known as tapping, is a valuable technique that can help you to release and reframe beliefs that aren't serving you. To find out more about this technique and how you can get started, check out the bonus resources where you can get started straight away.

Having acknowledged your beliefs, understood them and started the process of releasing them, let's look at finding forgiveness. Resentment can become a huge weight in your backpack, a mixture of anger, bitterness, and disappointment. Holding onto resentment is allowing that person, or event to maintain power over you. It continues to drain your energy, exaggerate negativity and keep you stuck. Letting go of that resentment and finding forgiveness is not about condoning other's actions. Instead, it's the conscious choice to let go and empower yourself to move forward. This is again something that can be achieved through tapping or perhaps writing a letter to the person you need to forgive. You can choose whether you send it. It can be cathartic to write the letter and then release by destroying it – a great excuse for a fire pit and perhaps a glass of wine.

The most challenging forgiveness is the forgiveness you give to yourself. You can find yourself holding onto the weight of past mistakes, regret and self-blame. It is time to show yourself the love and understanding to let go of these thoughts. Recognise that you are human and capable of mistakes. Undertake a visualisation to release yourself of the burden of self-blame. Picture yourself letting it go and allowing yourself to feel lighter. Hypnotherapy, EFT and meditation are all valuable ways to free yourself from these unnecessary burdens.

Forgiveness creates a space within you for more joy and positivity, enabling you to grow and move forward on your transformative journey. Each step you take lightens the load you have been carrying. Show yourself unconditional love and compassion to support yourself along the way.

In moments of overwhelm, when the inner critic is challenging you and the process, remember, it does this with love, not malice. Its intent is not to harm but to protect you from change. If you find yourself challenged, take a moment and remind yourself, it is all part of the journey and offer yourself some comfort. Acknowledge these difficult moments and provide yourself with the reassurance to know this is a moment in time and it is okay to feel this way because change can be unnerving, but that change is necessary to welcome a new chapter. Taking a proactive approach to your own well-being not only addresses that moment but also serves to reduce stress levels and improve your overall mental health, enhancing relationships and increasing your resilience.

When you are ready, let's continue exploring the processing and releasing of emotions. Just as you can fill your house with clutter, your mind and body can become overwhelmed with emotional clutter. Releasing your emotions is about acknowledging them, processing them and letting go - a topic already covered in Chapter Five.

Throughout this chapter, you have delved deep within and confronted past traumas, rewired limiting beliefs and released emotional clutter, providing yourself with love and compassion. In the following chapters, you will fill that space with positivity and define your vision for a happya life, exploring your unique recipe of happiness and contentment for living in alignment with your true self and achieving a sense of inner contentment, where clarity, purpose, fulfilment, and joy intertwine to create a lasting and enriched sense of well-being.

"The future belongs to those who believe in the beauty of their dreams."

— ELEANOR ROOSEVELT

CHAPTER 8

YES, TO YOUR DREAMS

As you get comfortable with who you are and how you are showing up for life with a greater awareness of what is truly important to you, and you begin to release the trauma from past chapters of your life, it's time to embark on a powerful journey to envision your happya life – a life filled with purpose, passion, and fulfilment, achieving your happya, a position of clarity, purpose, fulfilment and joy. It's time to dare to dream big. No longer do you need to hold onto beliefs that do not serve you. No longer are you a prisoner to judgement, shame and fear. Now's the time to reap the reward of all the hard work you have done, to celebrate and reward yourself by stepping into the arena and showing up for your dreams.

Embracing your vision empowers you to create the roadmap for your future and it helps you to stay focused when the jelly wobbles start to appear. Your vision acts as your compass, navigating you towards your desired destination and ensuring you don't get distracted and lost along the way. It's essential not to fill your vision with other's opinions on how your future life "*should*" look, hence leaving this piece of work until you had already set the foundations of knowing who you really are, acknowledging your past, letting go of limiting beliefs, establishing healthy boundaries and falling in love with who you really are. It must reflect who you are - your hopes, your passions and your values. If it isn't in alignment with you then it will never fulfil you and you will always be wondering why there isn't more. This is your time to be creative, to think outside the boundaries you have previously held yourself accountable to.

Don't allow your dreams to be limited by fear and self-doubt. In setting your vision for your future, ensure you have fully charged your batteries and are feeling empowered. Refer to Chapter Two and delve into your Happya Survival Kit to ensure you are on top form. Do something that makes you feel empowered. Refer to your survival kit and let's give you the supercharge you need to allow yourself to dream big.

You don't need to solve all the problems and answer all the questions of how you are going to get there right now, you just need to know that it is something you really want to achieve or have in your life. The thing is, if you don't have something you want in your sights then that is one sure way of ensuring you don't achieve it. So, be bold and brave and open to putting exactly what you want on your vision board because when the time comes, you will make the decision to make it happen. In the next chapter, we will be covering how to activate this into reality. Hold faith in the process.

If you were looking for proof it works, you are reading it right now. Four years ago, I rather sheepishly declared I'd love to publish a book and despite my inner voice saying to me *"You're never going to be able to do that"* (remember the limiting belief put in there when I was six years old?), I made the decision to write it on a Post-it note and stuck it on my vision board. It stayed there, fading in the sunlight from my office window. Each time I spotted it pinned on my wall, I began to get more comfortable with the possibility that one day, I would be a published author. I started to take notice of others publishing their books and seeing how their dreams were coming true. Then, my one day came. I was asked if I would be interested in co-authoring a book. It scared the pants off me, but I knew that this was my chance, this was my opportunity. This was the step I needed to take to enable me to recognise my potential and have the confidence to achieve my dream. So, I said yes. If it hadn't been for that post-it note, it would have been a missed opportunity.

Each step was scary, especially submitting my chapter to the editor. I mean, seriously, I was submitting it for the sole purpose of having it critiqued! Hadn't I already spent the last forty years suffering from the critique given when I was six? So, imagine my joy when the feedback was great, and that book went on to be a #1 best seller on Amazon. It was then I knew that one day, I was going to make this book a reality and here it is. A dream I never thought was possible all those years ago.

Now it's time for you to make *your* dream become *your* reality and the first step is acknowledging what it is you want to achieve.

Let's take a moment to remember the version of yourself that started on this journey, the moment you opened this book to begin reading. Think back to Chapter One when you looked in the mirror and made the decision that you wanted to get to know her - the moment you made the commitment to find your happya. Everything you have learned on this journey is going to equip you for the future success you desire. Everything you have experienced provides insight into what is important to you. Remember that journey, because in that journey lies the wisdom to support you as you venture towards your future. Your past is not a place to set up home, but a place to be held in your memory so you can do better next time. Now is the time to start mapping out your next chapter.

Firstly, let's consider why having a dream is important. Having a dream provides a sense of purpose that your actions have intent, and your life has meaning, which enhances your overall well-being. Next, having a dream is a powerful motivator - it provides direction and energises you to take action and overcome challenges you may face along the way. It particularly helps with resilience - having a dream and sense of purpose provides a reason to bounce back from adversity. Having clarity and direction is empowering and enhances positive emotions of joy and gratitude. Having a dream supports you in living in alignment with your values, improving your sense of identity. Overall, having a dream is a catalyst for well-being, resilience and personal growth. It is a significant feature of finding your happya.

So, what's stopping you? Unfortunately, it's not as easy as it might sound. It's not uncommon to find yourself in a position of knowing what you don't want but not being clear on what you do want. If that's the case, don't worry, you are not alone and as you have done throughout this book, you must trust yourself and trust the process.

To achieve your dreams, you first need to know what that dream is. It needs to be something that you connect with on a deeper level. Your dream is yours and yours alone. The only boundaries of limitation are those which you place upon yourself, unless, of course, it is not a scientific possibility and well, even then, who knows? There was a time when people thought the world was flat and eating carrots improved your night vision, so who knows what is possible? If it wasn't for visionaries, our world would look a very different place. So, what is your dream? What do you envisage to be the next chapter in your story? Clearly, you are looking for something "more", something that offers you satisfaction in life, that improves your overall well-being and offers contentment and fulfilment. If you weren't then you would have long since given up reading this book, but here you are.

Your dream or vision for your future is a complex picture that fulfils your needs and wants. In defining your vision, you will uncover your aspirations and create your happya life - a life aligned with your authentic self, your unique recipe of happiness and contentment. Your vision plays an essential part in creating your happya life. Imagine setting out on a journey with no idea where you're heading, without a map or sat nav. Your vision provides direction and purpose and brings a sense of meaning to your life. It provides clarity and purpose, helping you to understand what is important to you. It helps align your goals with your values and your passion, enabling you to focus your actions and gain momentum.

In the face of adversity and when your energy and attention are beginning to wane, a personal vision is a source of motivation that fuels your determination to overcome challenges, so you keep on going. It gives you the resilience you need to persevere. Positive psychology highlights the importance of having a sense of purpose and meaning and your vision provides the picture for this.

Not only does a vision support you in your future but it also forms part of your recovery process. Experiencing trauma can shatter the very foundations of your identity. A vision provides a focus that can lead you back to a sense of meaning and a renewed purpose. It can provide a sense of empowerment, putting you in control of your narrative and energising you with a sense of determination.

If you woke up tomorrow morning and you were happya, what would that feel like? Think about how you would wake up. Where would you be? What would your surroundings look like? What would you hear? Who would be around you? What time would it be? Go through every step thinking in detail about every aspect. Think about the types of products you would use and the clothes you would be wearing. Give as much consideration to how you would be feeling at each stage, the needs you have as well as your aspirations. Remember, there is no compromising, this is your vision. You may need to do this exercise for different days. Perhaps your weekend looks different to your week. Take your time in doing this exercise and repeat it several times to see how it evolves. Allow yourself to explore the possibilities. If you are more visual, then look for images that represent the lifestyle you want to have. You can do this online or physically by going through magazines. Create a vision board or have a dream box. Where would you holiday? What job would you do? How would you spend your time? Consider what happiness and contentment look like for you. What are your deepest desires? What would you like to achieve? Collect images, words and symbols that represent your goals and desires.

Revisit the personal mission statement you wrote in Chapter Four. Consider how your values will be upheld in your vision of a happya life. Challenge yourself to think big, consider what each of your desires would mean to you and how they would feel to achieve. Contemplate what you have noticed in the previous chapters as being important to you. Ensure you cover all aspects of your life. Consider your career, what would your professional life look like - include job satisfaction, career progression, work-life balance, salary and benefits? Reflect on your finances, not only your income but savings, budgeting and any financial goals including provisions for yourself and your family in the future. Importantly, consider your health and well-being. How would you prioritise your mental and physical health? Consider family relationships, time spent together, communication and support. Do this for friendships, too. Consider your own personal growth. Is there some learning you would like to do, knowledge or skills you would like to gain? How would you spend your leisure time? What would you be doing; what pursuits would bring you joy? How would you relax? Other areas for consideration would be the environment, your surroundings and your contribution to the wider community. Consider your emotions and how you would like to feel, the time you would dedicate to each of these different areas. How would you connect to your spirituality, your beliefs and values and gain a sense of inner peace? All these areas demand some consideration.

What is the thing that you are holding back from including? Have you got something that you have never shared before because you haven't considered it a possibility? Write it down. You can figure out the how later but even having the audacity to write it down will give you the very boost you need to be successful.

This is an exercise you can repeat several times, allowing the ideas to ferment over the coming days and weeks. Start a dream journal where you actively explore your aspirations - reflecting on reoccurring themes can reveal patterns and offer guidance if you are still struggling. Create a vision board and collect images, words, symbols and quotes that represent your dreams and aspirations. Having something visible, rather than words, can support you in connecting with your innermost desires. Consider individuals you admire, explore what inspires you about these people - what is it about their lifestyle you find desirable? Explore how this aligns with your own set of values. Imagine yourself being able to transport into the future, where would you see yourself? What would you have achieved? You can do this exercise for various stages in life. Perhaps consider yourself at forty, fifty, sixty, seventy, eighty... whatever is relevant for you.

Determining your vision and dreams requires considered self-reflection and awareness. To determine a meaningful vision, it must align with your core values and reflect what truly matters to you. It must evoke emotions of joy and ignite your passion and enthusiasm to ensure you are motivated to work towards its realisation. It must resonate with you emotionally and provide sufficient clarity so you can connect not only with what needs to be done but also with what it will offer you when achieved. It must consider all aspects of your life, ensuring balance. There will need to be an element of flexibility to allow for personal growth and it must hold personal significance. This must be your dream and not a vision that is held by others for you. By contemplating all these criteria, you can ensure your vision is not only compelling and in alignment, but also comprehensive. As you continue on this journey, your vision will adapt and grow and while some things will be achieved, you may realise that your vision needs to adapt as does your identity.

Whilst this chapter has offered an insight into how you can develop your own vision, as with everything in life it's not without its challenges. You will need to overcome some familiar hurdles to ensure what you are creating is something that truly inspires you and results in you finding your happya. If you aren't going to go all in, you can't expect to achieve total satisfaction. In essence, it isn't as simple as having a dream, you need to know what you want but you also must believe that you are able and worthy of achieving it. This is where you can find your self-limiting beliefs hinder your progress if they haven't been fully dealt with in the previous chapters. Negative beliefs about your worthiness or your capabilities will hinder your ability to create the vision and for some, this can be paralysing leaving you stuck. If you lack sufficient clarity to define your vision, you may want to get support in understanding your values or passions. Check back in with Chapter Four if you find your vision is not resonating with you. The biggest resistance is likely to be resistance to change, fear of the unknown and fear of failure. Your vision may call for some changes in your life, which can feel overwhelming. Remind yourself of the tools you have in your survival kit. If you are experiencing the fear of failure, remember that failure only happens when you give up trying. Sometimes, we need to take a wrong turn to see the right one. You have already come so far, and you didn't do all it takes to get here without being capable or deserving of your dreams. Each time you come up against a challenge, go back to the relevant chapter and revisit and revise the work you have done. You will find yourself constantly evolving and uncovering more about yourself and challenging yourself to take continual steps towards the achievement of your increasing aspirations as you realise your potential.

Remember, practise self-compassion, challenge the negative narrative and surround yourself with people who uplift you and who believe in your potential. The happya community is a safe and welcoming space for you to find others who are on this journey. Check out the bonus resources and find others who are on a similar path.

Your vision and your dreams provide the blueprint for your life, a life you have envisioned in connection with your true self. It reflects your deepest desires. Once you have identified what your future vision is, it's like planting the seeds of your future life. Once planted you must nurture and cultivate them empowering yourself to take the necessary actions to turn them into reality. The choices you make today determine your future potential. As the author of your own life, what story are you going to write? With vision comes clarity. When life ultimately challenges you; your vision remains your constant. Your vision becomes the light when life feels dark. You may need to take a different route, but the destination remains the same. Holding onto your vision provides purpose and passion, aligned with your authentic self, your vision gives you a direction in which to head. It also enhances your resilience to keep on going. You know your purpose and having a vision enables you to measure how far you've come.

Now you have that vision, you must believe in your capacity to achieve it. In Chapter Four, you were introduced to self-belief and how positive affirmations can help reinforce your self-belief. Look how far you have come already in increasing the belief you have in yourself to make change happen. Consider all you have achieved to date, including all you have overcome. This is just the next step on that journey. In the following chapter, we will be exploring how you can break this vision down into goals that are achievable and meaningful. Action is the bridge between dreams and reality. Ensure your vision is something that evokes passion inside and motivates you to keep on going and even in challenging times, you will be able to remain focused, even if that means taking a step back.

In summary, knowing your vision, believing in it and yourself, and finding the momentum and motivation to take positive action are your keys to success. Now, charge your batteries and let's get ready in the next chapter to take some action.

"Setting goals is the first step in turning the invisible into the visible."

— TONY ROBBINS

CHAPTER 9

ACTIVATE YOUR LIFE

I n the previous chapter, you defined your vision and connected with your dreams, now it's time to transform that vision into reality. It is time for you to take the steps necessary to activate your happya life. You have already come so far; this is just the next step on your journey. This chapter outlines how to turn that vision into actionable steps, the key success factors, the potential pitfalls to avoid and strategies to tackle setbacks.

Having defined your vision, it is time to start implementing change in your life. Perhaps something easier said than done. The important thing here is to remain connected to your vision and why it is important to you. Remember the commitment you made in setting out on this journey? This is the time to get really stuck in and, as mentioned in each chapter, dig deep into that survival kit and ensure your energy is charged for the next step.

Your vision, the dream life you envisage, may feel like it is a long way off but every step you take is a step closer to realising it and no matter how small that step, you will be closer than you were yesterday. Inevitably, there will be times when you may be thrown off course, when challenges arise but you keep on going because it is only inaction that will ensure you never make it, and you know you are worth more than that.

The first action is to break down your vision into the key areas of your life. These were mentioned in the previous chapter: finances, career, family, learning and personal development, spirituality, relationships, recreation and health. Don't worry if you have chosen different categories, use the categories you have chosen. For each of these key areas, make a commitment to what you want to achieve within a certain period. Perhaps it will be in the next three months, or even the next five years, whatever feels right for you. These commitments become the goals that you will focus upon over the given period. When planning your time and contemplating new opportunities, you will need to consider how it will affect the achievement of these goals.

For each of your goals, it's time to take a dual approach to creating actionable steps towards their attainment. Firstly, work backwards, taking a top-down approach. Start with where you want to be and then note what step comes beforehand, keep going with the process until you can't envision anymore and stop. Now, take a bottom-up approach, where you think of the next step to take towards your goals from today. This approach should help you bring the start and end points closer together and establish a clear roadmap. This may be a task you want to complete over time as often when getting into the detail of goals, you can begin to uncover more limiting beliefs and you will need to re-energise and spend time challenging them before you can move forward.

To be successful, you need to ensure you address any concerns raised by your inner self. This doesn't mean succumbing to the negative dialogue. As discussed in previous chapters, it's about hearing the messages and providing reassurance and compassion. By the end of the exercise, you should have a clear picture of the steps it will take you to achieve your goal. Ask yourself, as of today, what is the first step towards your goal, then the next, and the next. Really begin to imagine yourself succeeding every step of the way. If a step feels too big then break it down. Have you ever heard the saying, *"How do you eat an elephant? One bite at a time."*? It's all about taking small, achievable bites at your goals. If you find your emotions are starting to become overwhelming, revisit the exercises in Chapter Five and as always, use the tools and techniques you have in your survival kit.

In the setting and achievement of goals, there are five key success factors. Firstly, you need to have clarity about what you are trying to achieve. Be clear and specific. Think about what success looks like for you, what would bring you joy in achieving each stage? Connect with that emotion. Life is not just about what you think, it's also about what you feel. Set meaningful goals, considering how they translate into reality. Be as specific as possible so that on those days when you lack direction, your goals can still provide you with clarity and meaning.

Next, it takes commitment. To be successful in achieving your wants and desires, you must be prepared to go all in. Be honest with yourself about what you are prepared to commit to and how you will hold yourself accountable. What do you need to do to ensure you are successful? What will you need to start doing? What will you need to stop doing? Are you ready to make that commitment? Are you prepared to do what is necessary? If you find some resistance here, ask yourself whether this is a limiting belief you are holding onto or is it that the vision needs some adjustment, that it isn't quite what you wanted? It's okay to change your mind, just make the decision from a place of positive intent and not from a place of fear. When you are ready, it is time to declare your commitment. If you aren't ready to go public or find a confidante to hold you accountable, then it's down to you. Write your commitment out and keep it visible to you. Check in with it daily and embrace the opportunities that come your way. Having your goals and your commitment statement at the forefront of your mind will help you make aligned choices.

In actioning your goals, you will face challenges. To stay on track, be prepared for potential challenges. Give some thought in advance about where these may come from and consider issues you may have faced previously in working towards your goals. Acknowledging issues enables you to find resolutions with relative ease and predicting them may even allow you to avoid some of the pitfalls. Consider how you will maintain your energy when you do hit obstacles and how your survival kit can support you. For all your goals, consider what you need to know and learn to be successful, whether it's additional resources or information you will need to get the task done. Think about who can help you and who will be your cheerleaders along the way. You'll be surprised how empowering it is to know there is someone in your corner. Embrace a growth mindset and see challenges as opportunities for learning and personal development.

If you find yourself overwhelmed, reach into your survival kit and re-energise. Show yourself some compassion and self-love. If you find yourself stuck, consider those additional resources, take time to reflect when things go wrong and adjust accordingly. If you face challenges and setbacks, take what you can learn from them and grow. This is a marathon, not a sprint and you need to maintain a connection with the wider vision you hold for yourself and the commitment you made.

Next, it is important to remain focused and concentrate on your reasons for taking the step, what you are looking to achieve in your future life. Focus on the journey ahead of you, what you are moving towards and what achieving each step will mean to you. It is time for you to start showing up as the person you are hoping to become. Think about how the person you intend on becoming would show up and how they would behave. It is time to start taking action in the same way. It is the only way to achieve your goal. If you think about someone becoming an elite athlete, they don't start by saying when they become skilled enough, they will eat the right things and train the right amount. They first behave in the way that the person they want to become would behave, by following the routine and programmes to improve their fitness and stamina. When you go to a job interview, you behave and respond as though you are already capable and competent of doing the job. So, consider now how you need to be showing up and what habits and rituals can help you on the road to success. Identify the resources you will need to access to be successful, where you may need additional support and input and how you can gain access to these.

Inevitably, the key success factor is action. Reflect on your top three actions for the next few weeks. What would it mean to achieve these? If you had already accomplished them, how would you feel? What difference would they make to your life? Create the plan and start putting your goals into action. Reward yourself for the progress and success you achieve and show yourself compassion when you face setbacks. Embrace conscious decision-making and take intentional action. Remember, if your actions don't achieve the goal or you experience a diversion in your intended route, then it is not time to give up on your vision, you must look for an alternative way. You change the plan, not the dream. Think about if you were heading out on a journey; if you discovered the road was closed, you would find an alternative, you wouldn't just turn around and go home, so why do this with something that you have committed to being your happya life? Yes, it may take longer than you anticipated but you are the only one who's counting, there are no deadlines on your dreams.

As you venture on this transformative journey to realising your happya life, it is crucial to acknowledge the potential pitfalls that may arise. Having an awareness of them can empower you to navigate them with determination and increase your resilience, ensuring that setbacks simply become additional steps rather than blocking the road ahead. A common pitfall is the continuous effort that is required to achieve your goals and realising that the benefits may take time. It may take longer than you thought, and the journey may be harder. Prepare yourself and your energy for the road ahead by ensuring you have the strategies in place to maintain your energy packs with a fully-stocked survival kit.

Other pitfalls include the potential of self-doubt and limiting beliefs. Surrounding yourself with a support network will help you to navigate through these times. There will be moments when it will be important to lean on others. Ensure you have a community of people around you who support your dreams and protect yourself from those who may sabotage your efforts.

Inevitably, life can throw us curveballs and unexpected events may happen. Flexibility and adaptability are key to navigating unforeseen challenges without losing sight of your vision.

The biggest potential threat to your success is likely to be you and fear. Fear can hold you back, it can cause you to sabotage your efforts and can leave you paralysed. That fear is not just of failure, it can just as easily be a fear of success. Acknowledge the fear but don't give it power, show it compassion and if you fail, use it as part of your personal growth. You have found a way not to do it, so you are a step closer to getting it right next time.

Ultimately, set yourself on the right path by setting yourself up for success. Give yourself the resources and support you need, embrace the journey with its highs and lows and remember that every day, you are a step closer to your dreams.

In summary, to ensure you have clarity and alignment with your authentic self, you must be truly connected to your vision and why it holds so much relevance and significance to you. Next, commit to taking the right steps and putting in the work, giving yourself what you need to be successful. Be prepared for the challenges you will face and plan accordingly. Focus on your vision and what that means to you. Finally, act, take positive, deliberate action towards your vision. Hold belief in yourself and your abilities to make this happen. Look in that mirror and tell yourself each day that you've got this. When your inner critic rises, listen to her, reassure her that you've got this and remind her that you will never abandon her again.

You have your survival kit, this book, and the bonus resources, if you get stuck you can always reach out to the happya community for support. You are not alone in these challenges; we are here to help, and we are along for the journey.

"The book may end but survival was just the beginning; the rest of the story is yours to create."

— CLARE DEACON

CONCLUSION
EMBRACING YOUR JOURNEY TO A HAPPYA LIFE

Congratulations on getting to the end of this book and for persevering on your journey even when it may have become uncomfortable and other activities could have become so much more appealing. Congratulations on all the effort you have put in, the key learnings you have made and the steps you have taken towards creating your happya life. It is time to acknowledge the effort you have put into the process and how far you have come. Take a moment to go back to the commitment you made in Chapter One. Think about the feelings and emotions you had when you wrote that commitment - the expectations you had for the journey. Undoubtedly, there will be areas where you have made progress whilst in other areas, perhaps you feel you need more support or perhaps your anticipation was a little different. Either way, all information and emotions are good to acknowledge. For the areas that fell short of expectations, think about what you were missing, what need wasn't met and how can you fill that going forward. Then think about all that you have achieved, and reflect on what was different, what resonated along the journey, enabling you to succeed. Connect with your emotions and take that learning to continue growing.

Consider each of the chapters and what you have taken away from them. In chapter one, you were introduced to the power of belief and how it determines the difference between achieving growth and living a happya life or remaining stuck in survival with a sense of helplessness. It covered how the concept of normal impacts your well-being and how important it is to recognise and embrace your unique identity.

In Chapter Two, you were introduced to the concept of well-being as being a state of contentment and fulfilment, a place where your individuality can bloom, and the importance of self-care. Hopefully, you have packed your survival kit and have recognised your needs to ensure your well-being and your energy packs are proactively managed and maintained. Make sure you continue your commitment to maintaining your self-care by giving yourself the compassion you so rightly need and deserve. Your survival kit is vital in your ongoing transformation and personal development.

Having packed your survival kit, we then explored the story of your journey in Chapter Three. We discussed the significance of trauma on your life and the backpack of experiences you carry along with you. The chapter concluded by recognising that you are the author of your story, and you get to decide how you carry your past and the next chapter that you write.

We subsequently delved into self-discovery in Chapter Four, Harmonising Your Authenticity. We explored your values and passions and what held meaning and purpose. We sought to uncover the inner you - the one that has been hidden beneath layers of limiting beliefs and others' expectations. The chapter reconnected you with your authentic self so you could begin the process of building a life attached to who you really are. Take a moment to reflect on how you have reconnected with your authentic self. What have been the key learnings? How have you been acknowledging who you really are and how have others responded to you showing up as your true self?

In acknowledging your emotions in Chapter Five, we explored your emotions, seeking to gain clarity of the messages they hold and acknowledging them rather than trying to avoid them, accepting the wisdom, they bring and learning how to manage them effectively so that you can find an improved sense of emotional stability. Gaining control over your emotions will enable you to navigate your life with purpose, in alignment with your authentic self.

Next, we explored preserving your space in Chapter Six, ensuring you upheld your boundaries and surrounded yourself with a supportive network. Consider the relationships you have nurtured and cultivated. How has your network changed? How have they uplifted and inspired you? Reflect in these concluding pages how significant your community is and recognise how you will continue to maintain your boundaries as you continue your journey.

In Chapter Seven, we reflected on your self-limiting beliefs. What were the things that were holding you back from living the life you wanted? What were the things you needed to let go of? Take a moment to reflect on the work that still needs to be done. How have you let go of some of those beliefs and what do you still need to work on?

Having reconnected and gained a better understanding of who you truly are and how you got to this time in your life, we ventured into your dreams, creating a vision of your future life and the achievement you aspire toward in Chapter Eight.

In Chapter Nine, we then translated that passion into action so you could plot the journey that you need to take in concluding this book. We developed your actionable steps, identified the key success factors, recognised the potential pitfalls, and considered the strategies to adapt when facing setbacks.

It may be the final chapter of this book, but this is not the end of your journey. Your personal transformation is a continuous one and happya is here to support you. Reflect on the transformative nature of the journey and celebrate your achievements. Now you are equipped with the knowledge and understanding you need to further pursue your own happya life. No doubt, there are still areas for you to explore and as you achieve your goals, your mind will inevitably open further to the belief that you have the potential for more. Your identity is not static, it is a living and evolving entity and to maintain your well-being requires a journey of lifelong learning and supporting yourself with the tools and techniques you have packed in your survival kit.

New opportunities will come your way along with life's challenges, but you are now better equipped to process them and continue your journey. Hopefully, now you have recognised that you are worthy of living a life in alignment with your true self and that you and your life are a gift waiting to be explored and celebrated.

For all the work you have already done throughout this journey, you are going to have to continue to put in that effort so that you never get stuck again. Each time you do the work, you will find it easier to dig deeper and you will notice how you are naturally upholding your boundaries, how you are challenging your inner critic and importantly, how you are showing up for yourself. Maintain your self-worth and give yourself the self-love and compassion you so rightly deserve. There will be times when you slip, you will fail, and you will make mistakes. What counts is what you do about it. Learn and grow so you can go on to flourish and thrive. Now, it's over to you.

Stay connected with the happya community for ongoing support and exclusive content on your path to a happya life of contentment and fulfilment. Thank you for allowing me to be a part of your journey.

Join Our Happya Life Community

Having read the final chapter of this transformative journey, you're not just concluding your reading; you're embarking on a whole new chapter of your own happya life. It has been a privilege to accompany you on this path, and we want you to know that your interaction with happya doesn't need to end here.

The happya life community is a place where individuals like you, seeking healing and happiness, come together to share their journeys, offer support, and find inspiration. It's a welcoming space where compassion and empathy are abundant and the pursuit of a happya life is celebrated.

We extend a warm welcome for you to become a part of our community. By joining us, you'll receive our newsletter, packed with insights, valuable resources and updates. If you've enjoyed the wisdom within these pages, you'll find even more to love in The Happya Life podcast and if you're hungry for knowledge, our Happya Life Blog awaits your exploration. Access to all this and so much more can be found by visiting our website at www. happyacoach.com.

We understand that your journey is unique, and there may be moments when you desire some personal guidance and support. Whether you are facing a specific challenge, seeking clarity or wish to delve deeper into the principles outlined in this book, remember, happya is only a message away. Reach out whenever you're ready, and we'll be honoured to guide you further on your path to a happya life.

We eagerly anticipate continuing to walk this path alongside you. Stay in touch and may your happya life journey continue to unfold, providing you with that sense of inner contentment, where clarity, purpose, fulfilment and joy intertwine to create a lasting enriched sense of well-being – a state far beyond survival.

Mental Health Resources

Organisations and Hotlines:

1. Samaritans

Website: www.samaritans.org

Call: 116 123

The Samaritans offer emotional support 24 hours a day, 365 days a year – in full confidence.

2. MIND

Website www.mind.org.uk

Call: 0300 123 3393

Mind offers an Infoline providing information and signposting service where you can talk to them about mental health problems and where you can get help. However, this is not a crisis line.

3. Anxiety UK

Website: www.anxietyuk.org.uk

Call: 03444 775 774

Anxiety UK offers a range of support services designed to help control anxiety rather than letting it control you.

4. Refuge

Website: www.nationaldahelpline.org.uk

Call: 0808 2000 247

Refuge is for women experiencing any kind of domestic abuse and concerned friends, family and colleagues looking to support someone who may be experiencing domestic abuse.

Talk to your GP may about your mental health problems to discover what services are available locally. For information from the NHS check out www.nhs.uk/mental-health.

Remember, reaching out for support is a sign of strength, not weakness. If you or someone you know is struggling with mental health issues, don't hesitate to seek help from these resources and individuals who are here to support you on your journey to well-being.

Bonus Material

Welcome, and congratulations on taking the first step towards your happya by reading this book. I'm excited to offer you a special bonus to support you further in implementing the steps within "Blooming Happya".

How to Access Your Free Bonuses:

1. **Visit Our Website:** www.happyacoach.com/ bloomingbonus where you'll discover a dedicated page where you can enter your email address.
2. **Check Your Inbox:** Once you've signed up, check your inbox, and ensure you whitelist our email to ensure you receive our messages without any issues.
3. **Access Your Resources:** After confirming your subscription, you'll receive immediate access to your bonus materials – all conveniently delivered straight to your inbox.

REMEMBER, YOUR JOURNEY IS JUST BEGINNING.

Your commitment to your personal growth and happiness is something worth celebrating and we're here to help you every step of the way.

Thank you for selecting to embark on this journey with happya. We firmly believe that everyone has the potential to grow, flourish and thrive, and to embrace their unique happya® life. Here's to your happiness, well-being, and a life harmoniously aligned with your authentic self.

With gratitude

Clare xx

Clare Deacon

Author Blooming Happya: Grow, Flourish, Thrive – Beyond Survival

Founder of Happya Ltd.